YALE STUDIES IN ENGLISH

Benjamin Christie Nangle, Editor

VOLUME 130

Satiric Allegory: Mirror of Man

ELLEN DOUGLASS LEYBURN

New Haven

YALE UNIVERSITY PRESS

London: Geoffrey Cumberlege, Oxford University Press

1956

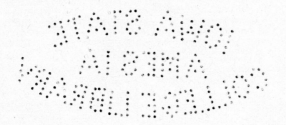

To

EMMA MAY LANEY

Teacher and Friend

Preface

THE CONVICTION on which the present study is based—that if satires cast in allegorical form are to be considered as works of art, they must be considered as allegories—is the outgrowth of years of teaching and studying many of the works in question. Consequently, it is impossible to acknowledge all the impressions in reading and conversation which have contributed to my thinking about them. Specific literary indebtedness is indicated in the notes; but I am grateful for many more sources of stimulation than I can name.

The holders of the copyrights have graciously allowed me to quote from the following works: Lucien Harris, from *Nights with Uncle Remus;* Harcourt, Brace and Company, from *Animal Farm* by George Orwell, copyright 1946; Brandt and Brandt, from *Nineteen Eighty-four* by George Orwell, copyright 1949 by Harcourt, Brace and Company; and Harper and Brothers, from *Brave New World* by Aldous Huxley. Paul Pickrel has kindly permitted me to quote from his unpublished Yale dissertation, "Religious Allegory in Medieval England."

I am grateful to the administration of Agnes Scott College, and particularly to President Wallace M. Alston, for sympathetic concern for the book and for allowing me a year's leave from academic responsibilities in which to bring it to completion.

The final writing was made possible by a research fellowship at the Henry E. Huntington Library, where the staff was unfailingly helpful. I should like especially to thank Godfrey Davies, Director of Research, for my election as fellow and for his encouragement and interest. The editors have kindly granted me permission to use in considerably altered form material on *Gulliver* and on *Hudibras* which first appeared in *The Huntington Library Quarterly.*

My greatest debt is to the following friends who have read the manuscript in various stages and made helpful suggestions: Page Ackerman, Grace Calder, Helen L. Gardner, George P. Hayes, Margaret Hodgen, Emma May Laney, Douglas V. Steere, H. T. Swedenberg, Jr., and Chauncey B. Tinker; and to Florence E. Smith, without whose painstaking work on proofs and index the printer's schedules could not have been met.

ELLEN DOUGLASS LEYBURN

Agnes Scott College
Decatur, Georgia

Contents

I

Definitions

"It is one of the maxims of civil law that definitions are hazardous."
SAMUEL JOHNSON

SATIRIC allegory has been more often written than written about. In current critical terminology, the word allegorical is almost synonymous with dull. The disparagement of allegory which began with Coleridge, or one might even say with Dr. Johnson, has continued unabated among distinguished critics who sometimes agree in little else except the judgment that allegory is lifeless and mechanical. "Allegory still continues to be used as a rhetorical device from time to time, but there is no voice heard in its praise." [1] By its very mildness, this statement of the prevailing opinion indicates how fixed is the attitude that allegory is a literary form hardly worth bothering about. The critics who expound the allegorical works of earlier periods are likely to begin with the assumption that their first task is to explain the taste of other days for such writing, to show why a work of the imagination should have been cast in allegorical form at all.

The status of satire is, of course, quite different. It has never been described by that most damning of critical adjectives *dull;* and it has of late had eloquent defenders against 19th-century charges of pre-occupation with evil and vituperation. One no longer hears such diatribes against it as those in which the Victorians so vindictively denounced it as vindictive. There have recently been serious reassessments of its essential moral purpose and many careful analyses of the artistic pro-cedure in particular works of satire. But since allegory has not shared in this return of Satire to a position among the Muses, there has been only the most cursory attention to the allegory in allegorical satires. Perhaps it is not being too allegorical to suggest that there is also a Muse of Allegory; and furthermore that the Muse of Satire and the Muse of Allegory must be one if they are to preside successfully over a work of allegorical satire.

1. Joshua McClennen, "On the Meaning and Function of Allegory in the English Renaissance," *University of Michigan Contributions in Modern Philology, 1,* No. 6 (1947), 1.

The first problem which confronts the critic of satiric allegory is that of making clear to himself and to his reader just what he is talking about. What is sadly to seek is any rhetoric of the form, or even any acknowledgment that it exists as a form. Defense must therefore begin with definition. But allegory is one of the most difficult of critical terms to define; and satire is not much easier. The difficulty is more than doubled when they are put together since there is a persistent feeling that they do not belong together at all. Every one uses the words allegory and satire and thinks he knows what he means by them, but he often fails to communicate his meaning to a hearer who understands them quite differently. The very commonness of the terms and the looseness with which they are used make them hard to define; and the feeling that they are antithetical complicates the treatment of their union in satiric allegory.

Another complication comes from the shifts of dominant meanings from age to age. These are perhaps more marked in satire than in allegory. Nobody would now insist on Hall's criteria of a set verse form and a rough manner for satire, whereas the idea that personified abstraction is essential to allegory still appears in handbooks and dictionaries. But confusions of outworn usage hover over satire too; and even the old association of fierceness with formal verse satire clings to the term itself because of the fresh vitality given by Meredith's invidious distinction between satire and comedy to the notion of satire as a direct blow, a slap in the face. The retaining of outmoded conceptions not clearly distinguished in use from the new ones in the gradual shifts of language contributes something to the richness of satire and allegory, but it is a rich confusion. Ambiguity, both in a pejorative sense and in the sense of layers of meaning brought into high repute by Empson and the new critics, marks the use of both terms. The folly of trying to fix language is patent. As Johnson remarked in the preface to the Dictionary: "to enchain syllables, and to lash the winds are equally the undertakings of pride, unwilling to measure its desires by its strength." But in the spirit of the exhortation with which he concludes his survey of the difficulty of definition, "Let us make some struggles for our language," it may be possible to cut a path through the thicket of conflicting notions of satire and allegory to some definition that seems to fit the examples which give meaning to the term allegorical satire. Definition may provide some criteria by which to judge the works in question as works of art.

To begin then with allegory, the term in sadder disrepute. At least the origin of the word is clearer than that of the word satire; and we gain something by remembering that ἀγορεύω indicates a speech made in the agora and that ἄλλος is the adjective *other*. Thus the idea of deliberate dissimulation in a public speech is in ἀλληγορία. This meaning of doubleness is all that is conveyed by Quintilian, Cicero, or Plutarch, or by the medieval grammarians and Renaissance writers of dictionaries and rhetorics who derive from them. *Aliud verbis, aliud sensu* is the phrase that recurs in their definitions. A typical definition is that of Richard Sherry, "Allegoria, quae est oratio aliud verbis, aliud sensu demonstrans." [2] But the treatments of the uses of allegory in Renaissance criticism show that the long practice of it by the Middle Ages has had its effect upon the conception of the term, however strictly the actual definitions still adhere to Quintilian's statement. It has come to be considered as morally useful, its function being purely didactic. Aesthetic considerations are entirely subordinate. What charm the surface image has is judged by its effectiveness in charming the reader into truth. This function of allegory becomes in Sidney's *Defence of Poesie* a part of the larger justification of poetry itself, which must be made the hand-maiden of morality.

The strong conviction of the Renaissance writers that allegory is a decoration of unpalatable truth, the sugar coating of the pill, seems a direct outgrowth of just one branch of its use during the Middle Ages. The medieval church had made a variety of uses of allegory. Its importance in the interpretation of scripture is indicated by its presence in three of the four senses, literal, allegoric, tropologic, and anagogic, referred to in the familiar rime:

> Littera gesta docet;
> Quid credas allegoria.
> Moralis quid agas;
> Quo tendas anagogia.

How strongly allegorical were all the senses except the literal is simply demonstrated by the example given in the article on Exegesis in *The Catholic Encyclopedia,* which explains that Jerusalem is literally the Holy City; allegorically, the Church Militant; tropologically (morally), the just soul; and anagogically (prophetically), the Church Triumphant. Dante's setting forth of the various senses is as revealing of the medieval habit of interpretation as of his own intention in *The Divine Comedy*.

The use of allegory in the service of morality could obviously be either reproof or edification. Often, as in the countless wars of the vices and virtues for the soul of man, it could be both at once. Furthermore, the medieval instructor in morals often made use simultaneously of symbol and personification. The proliferation of personified abstractions in medieval works is probably responsible for the gradual linking of personification with the definition of allegory. This has been one of the most confusing developments in the usage of the word, for there is nothing inherently allegorical about personification. The remoteness of

2. *A Treatise of the Figures of Grammer and Rhetoricke* (London, 1555), p. ciiii.

personification from allegory before the association developed in the Middle Ages is indicated by the fact that Quintilian discusses them in different books of the *Institutio Oratoria.* Indeed, the naming of an abstraction is contrary to the essential conception of concealment which is basic in allegory. There is no veiling, either for purposes of intensification or of actual hiding of meaning, in calling a quality by name. Allegory begins only when the quality is set in motion. Abstractions cannot act except metaphorically; thus in the medieval wars of the vices and virtues, it is the battles which are allegorical. The inactive capitalized abstractions of much 18th-century poetry are not allegorical at all. But the usurpation of the word allegory by personification and the assumption that personification is bound to be mechanical have been more responsible than any other development for the disrepute into which the term began to fall in the late 18th century and from which it is only beginning to emerge. The disparagement of allegory among the new critics, who have written so illuminatingly of metaphor, is largely the result of this strange appropriation of the word by one of the forms it has taken, and that not an essential one. What is essential to it is indirection, which is also essential to metaphor. It is a work of the imagination, a conveying of one thing in terms of another quite as actually as is metaphor.

A concomitant of the preoccupation with personification is the feeling that elevation rather than reproof by a demonstration of evil is the function of allegory. This is a misconception which is particularly bothersome in a consideration of the affinity between allegory and satire. But almost universal as the notion now is in handbooks and encyclopedias, it is a late development. Renaissance critics concentrate almost exclusively on the moral usefulness of allegory, as if the truth which it is designed to make the patient swallow would of necessity be unpalatable without the sugar coating. There is a good deal of emphasis in the 17th century on the disapproval of allegory as misleading, a point of view more than once expressed in earlier criticism: "Now to Discourse of the Natures of Things in Metaphors and Allegories is nothing else but to sport and trifle with empty words, because these Schems do not express the Natures of Things, but only their Similitudes and Resemblances, for Metaphors are only words, which properly signifying one thing, are apply'd to signifie another by reason of some Resemblance between them." [3] It is not until the 18th century that the idea of exaltation becomes firmly linked with allegory. It develops at the same time with an increased emphasis upon aesthetic appeal. More than one 18th-century critic gives rules for making allegory pleasing and

---

3. Samuel Parker, *A Free and Impartial Censure of the Platonick Philosophie* (Oxford, 1666), p. 74. Quoted by George Williamson, "The Restoration Revolt against Enthusiasm," *Studies in Philology, 30* (1933), 593.

points out the difficulty of handling the form. Joseph Priestley, for instance, declares that "It requires uncommon skill and caution to conduct a long allegory with propriety; because few things are analogous
in many respects, at the same time that they are sufficiently different
to make the analogy pleasing. Moreover, it is very difficult to make an
allusion intelligible, and at the same time never name the thing we
mean in direct terms, which we must by all means avoid; as it would
introduce the greatest confusion into the metaphor."[4] Throughout
the century in definitions of allegory, little is said about personification
because it seems to be assumed. The definition in Johnson's Dictionary,
which may be taken as representing the view of the time, includes in
its example the idea of personification: "A figurative discourse, in which
something other is intended, than is contained in the words literally
taken; as, *wealth is the daughter of diligence, and the parent of authority.*" Before the attack of the romantic critics upon allegory, then,
the associations with it of personification and elevation were fixed.

Another accretion to the conception of allegory, if not to its definition, is the feeling that a story, or at least some action, is essential. This
too may result from the prominence of personification in allegory.
Since it is only by acting that abstractions become allegorical at all,
there must be action if the work in which they appear is to exist as
allegory. But there is no hint of the need of a story in early definitions;
and indeed 20th-century definitions may suggest alternatives to narrative, as does the one: "sustained description or narration, treating
directly of one subject, but intended as an exposition of another."[5]
There can, I think, be no justification for making narrative a criterion
of allegory, though certainly many allegories have depended on the
representing of one series of actions in terms of another. Nor can
length be considered essential, though many allegories are long.

The commonest definition in current handbooks and dictionaries is
"sustained metaphor"; but the word "sustained" in this definition needs
clarification. What is essential to the existence of allegory is a pattern
of relationship in both tenor and vehicle.[6] Some relationship, whether
narrative or other, must be sustained at both levels of meaning if the
allegory is to exist at all, in contrast to metaphor which it otherwise so

4. *A Course of Lectures on Oratory and Criticism* (London, 1777), p. 195.

5. The rest of the definition, from the *Jewish Encyclopedia,* indicates the fixity of the
idea of elevation: "the latter having a more spiritual nature than the former, yet bearing
some resemblance to it. It is a comparison between two different groups of ideas on the
basis of something possessed in common. It has for its purpose the illustration or in-
culcation of a higher truth."

6. Cf. the definition given by Paul Pickrel: "It presents a group of vehicles (things
expressed) corresponding to a group of tenors (things behind the things expressed),
and the vehicles stand for a pattern of relationship and (usually) engage in a pattern
of activity corresponding to a like pattern of activity among the tenors." "Religious
Allegory in Medieval England" (Yale dissertation, 1944), p. 13.

closely resembles. We can, then, call allegory the particular method of
saying one thing in terms of another in which the two levels of meaning
are sustained and in which the two levels correspond in pattern of
relationship among details.

In terms of this definition, it is possible to establish several criteria
for judging allegory in general and satiric allegory in particular. In
accordance with it, both patterns of relationship are to be self-
consistent. The surface level should be clear and interesting on its own
plane; but since its reason for being is its illuminating something else,
it must have enough resemblance to let us know what is signified as
well as enough difference to engage us imaginatively. It is in the interrelations of tenor and vehicle that the peculiar interest of allegory consists. There must be likeness enough to make the reader feel that the
use of one to stand for the other is legitimate, and also to guarantee
that the elect will perceive the hidden meaning. Puttenham makes this
criterion part of his definition: "But properly & in his principall vertue
Allegoria is when we do speake in sence tranlatiue and wrested from the
owne signification, neuerthelesse applied to another not altogether contrary, but hauing much cõueniencie with it as before we said of
metaphore:" [7] Even when fear or snobbishness moves the writer to
use allegory actually to hide his meaning from improper readers, he
wants to be understood by his proper audience. The riddle which is
never guessed is no pleasure even to its propounder. And Quintilian
long ago condemned the allegory which was merely a riddle. On the
other hand, if the likeness between tenor and vehicle is too great, we
lose the specific allegorical pleasure of having the imagination actively
engaged. Lord Kames showed understanding of human nature when
he remarked: "we are pleased with the discovery because it is our own
work." [8] Moreover, likeness and difference must so interact as to make
each level gain something from the other. The pleasure in the image
depends on its being the image of something; nor is the something exactly what it would be without the image. The interaction of tenor and
vehicle makes them contribute to each other. Thus the fascination of the
form consists in its engaging both imagination and intellect. It at once
presents a riddle and lets us into the secret.

In the attempt to define satire, etymology is of little help, though
there is charm in the notion of the *lanx satura,* the dish of mixed fruit
offered to the gods, as well as in the fancy dear to the Elizabethans of
the criticism of human folly presented through satyrs. *Satura* does at
least convey the idea of variety which is characteristic of satire. One of

7. George Puttenham, *The Arte of English Poesie,* ed. Gladys Doidge Willcock and
Alice Walker (Cambridge, 1936), pp. 186–7.

8. Henry Home, Lord Kames, *Elements of Criticism* (Edinburgh and London, 1762),
3, 112.

the quirks of usage which makes the word hard to define is that it refers now to a form and now to an attitude. One critic attempting to bring precision to the matter creates four categories of terminology, which rather call attention to the complexity than resolve it: "the term *satirical spirit* . . . refers to a point of view; the word *satire* to a concrete but general embodiment of that point of view in literature; and *Satire* (capitalized) to the literary form or genre, as well as to any particular example of that genre." [9] Hall and his followers thought they were writing in a fixed genre with laws which very much complicated their enterprise; but Horace, one of the Romans whom they thought they were following, in writing about his art in the fourth and tenth satires of Book I, is talking about the purpose and feeling of his laughing criticism. Indeed, these urbanely modest little verse essays give the clue to the two criteria which may serve to bring together the many diverse conceptions of satire. There is always a judgment of faults, and there is always some sort of indirection in the conveying of the judgment, whether the concealment is laughter or some sterner sort of rhetorical intensification. Indirection as a basic necessity of good satire has been so ably set forth in recent criticism that there is no need to insist on it here except as it leads the satirist to choose allegory as a way of achieving fictionality. Even invective, if it is to be called satire and not mere abuse, must make some sort of appeal to the imagination. The further the satirist moves toward imaginative expression of his judgment, the more natural allegory appears as an artistic medium. Perhaps the Elizabethan idea of using the grotesque satyrs "so that they might wiselye vnder the abuse of that name, discouer the follies of many theyr folish fellow citesens," [1] is after all helpful in representing allegorically the definitive qualities of satire: judgment and indirection.

Further examination of these qualities with the criteria that arise from them is profitable in a consideration of satiric allegory. The essential nature of satiric allegory springs from the characteristics which allegory and satire have in common. Paramount among these is the quality of indirection, which is the definitive mark of allegory and which must in some sort mark satire as well. Another requisite of effective satire and effective allegory alike is the impression of economy, which comes from intensification. Yet this intensification is combined in both with the impression of detachment on the part of the author which leaves the reader a free agent. A further likeness is the conveying in each of the general by the particular with the consequent problems

9. Samuel Marion Tucker, *Verse Satire in England before the Renaissance* (New York, 1908), p. 3.
1. Thomas Lodge, "Defence of Poetry," *Elizabethan Critical Essays*, ed. G. Gregory Smith (Oxford, 1904), *I*, 80.

of adjustment: the sustaining of distinctness of levels and the degree of likeness between them. These similarities in artistic considerations suggest a basic resemblance in purpose, which indeed exists. Both allegorist and satirist are concerned to teach; the object of the artistry of each is to win over the reader to his point of view or to enforce a point of view which the reader already shares. Thus the affinity between allegory and satire is so strong that their occasional union in satiric allegory would seem inevitable.

The union has, in fact, been more than occasional. Satire seems always to have had a propensity toward allegorical form. The number of satirists from Lucian to George Orwell, not to name those now writing, who have turned to allegory as a mode of expression demonstrates the strength of the affinity. Yet curiously enough, in defiance of the evidence of one satire after another which is also an allegory, critics write as if there were something incongruous in the two. How foreign this impression of incongruity was to ancient rhetoricians is indicated by Quintilian's including irony and mockery, which we link with satire, under the kinds of allegory. But nowadays satire is thought of as preoccupied with the ugly and degraded aspects of human nature; allegory, with the beautiful and exalted. Satire looks down; allegory looks up. To put them together is, in the popular opinion, to achieve a sort of squint. A typical statement of the supposed opposition asserts: "The allegorical form is essentially constructive and didactic, and hence unfitted in its very nature for satirical purposes. It is also too abstract, while satire is essentially realistic." [2] But the allegory may be exactly the satirist's way of making his satire real, if not realistic.

It is the necessity of indirection, the mask that at once hides and reveals, which more than any other artistic consideration brings satire and allegory together. The importance of indirection for imaginative communication springs from the very nature of art. If we accept the idea of art as expression, we see at once the necessity of indirection. "This is why, as literary critics well know, the use of epithets in poetry, or even in prose where expressiveness is aimed at, is a danger. If you want to express the terror which something causes, you must not give it an epithet like 'dreadful.' For that describes the emotion instead of expressing it, and your language becomes frigid, that is inexpressive, at once. A genuine poet, in his moments of genuine poetry never mentions by name the emotions he is expressing." [3]

A recurring image for the effect of both satire and allegory is that of the mirror. The titles of such satires as *Speculum Stultorum* and *The Steele Glas* suggest it; and Barclay sets it forth in the Argument to *The Shyp of Foles:* "this our Boke representeth vnto the iyen of the

2. Tucker, *Verse Satire*, p. 72.
3. R. G. Collingwood, *The Principles of Art* (Oxford, 1938), p. 112.

redars the states and condicions of men: so that euery man may behold within the same the cours of his lyfe and his mysgouerned maners, as he sholde beholde the shadows of the fygure of his visage within a bright Myrrour." [4] What the mirror reveals is, to be sure, just a reflection of reality; but it is only by means of the reflection that reality is to be perceived. Swift is less sanguine than Barclay about the use of the mirror for self-scrutiny; but he keeps the conception of satire as a mirror: "*Satyr is a sort of Glass, wherein beholders do generally discover everybody's Face but their Own; which is the chief Reason for that kind Reception it meets in the World, and that so very few are offended with it.*" [5] The figure of the mirror is even more familiar to describe the use of metaphorical representation in poetry. Kenneth Burke relates its effect to the myth of Perseus and the Medusa with the protection which the mirror offers in the slaying of the monster. [6] Though he is discussing poetic indirection, his application of the myth is peculiarly suggestive of satire. The appropriation of the same figure of the mirror by both satire and metaphor, with the implied extension to allegory, indicates a fundamental affinity in the need for indirect communication through the reflection in the mirror. To say one thing in terms of another is the readiest way for the satirist to create the reflection and thus achieve artistic removal. Such removal is what gives his reader the chance to enjoy instead of resenting what Dryden in the preface to *Absalom and Achitophel* calls the sweetness which "tickles even while it hurts," since "no man can be heartily angry with him who pleases him against his will." If the victims of Dryden's satirical portraits were indeed pleased, the reason must have been the pleasure in making the adjustment of the pictures, the being allowed to create their own work of art, to play with the artist the game of indirection. The reader must participate for communication to take place; and his own activity is what makes for him the work of art.

The indirection which is of the essence of both satire and allegory, the element of expression without which they cannot exist, is also the instrument of artistic economy. Conciseness is one of the chief artistic aims of the satirist. Horace, in the tenth satire, makes brevity one of the criteria of the genre; but what is essential is not so much actual brevity as the effect of speed and compactness. Diffuseness is the shoal on which many a satire has foundered. It is likewise a danger for allegory. In view of the length of most medieval allegories, it may seem strange to claim economy as one of the qualities of allegory; but the tedious drawing out of endless ramifications of a figure is the

4. Ed. T. H. Jamieson (Edinburgh and London, 1874), *1, 17*.
5. Author's Preface to *The Battle of the Books* in *A Tale of a Tub &*, ed. A. C. Guthkelch and D. Nichol Smith (Oxford, 1920), p. 215.
6. *The Philosophy of Literary Form* (Baton Rouge, 1941), p. 63.

result of the medieval habit of mind and sometimes also of the inept-
ness of the writer, not of anything inherent in allegory. Whatever force
these allegories have, at least for the modern reader, comes from the im-
mediacy of the impact, from the concrete representation to the imagination, which intensifies the image whether the aim of the allegorist is
more to reveal or more to conceal by his outward figure. The similar
need of the satirist for some way of speaking to the imagination, for
expression in short, directs him to concreteness even when the concreteness is not allegorical. But allegory furnishes him one of the aptest
means to be concrete and thus economical, for it immediately engages
the activity of the reader.

It is one of the paradoxes of artistic response that economy is increased by what David Worcester calls the "time-lag." [7] The brief interval in which the reader makes the adjustment between the apparent
meaning and the real one is the moment when he is artist, when his
participation is most active. Thus when the adjustment is made, he has
a feeling of triumph that actually quickens response. The indirection
which compels the search of the imagination and its consequent leap
into the significance of the allegory or satire—or allegorical satire—
immensely sharpens the impact. The valuable cooperation between
the time-lag and actual economy is set forth in a little allegory by
Rabelais as a justification of the larger allegory in *Gargantua and
Pantagruel:* "you must, by a sedulous lecture, and frequent meditation,
break the bone, and suck out the substantial marrow; that is, my
allegorical sense." [8] But the substance is worth the sucking.

The same quality which makes for economy by throwing the responsibility on the reader and thereby quickening his imaginative response
enables the writer to hide behind his figure and let the reader draw his
own conclusions. There is a beguiling simplicity about allegory as a
means of making satire apparently objective. The writer can direct the
point of view without being present. He can give the impression of being
a fair and impartial presenter of evidence even while he is a judge controlling judgment. When Erasmus says to Sir Thomas More in the Preface to *The Praise of Folly:* "unless self-love deceives me badly, I have
praised folly in a way not wholly foolish," he is commenting not just on
his own allegorical representation of Folly praising herself, but on a controlling desire of the writer not to be called a fool for his pains. Neither
allegorist nor satirist wishes to betray himself and lay himself open to his
own exposure. C. H. Herford condemns the satire of Lydgate with an apt
phrase, "unseasonable earnestness," [9] that breaks in and dispels the il-

7. *The Art of Satire* (Cambridge, Mass., 1940), pp. 29–30.
8. Tr. Thomas Urquhart and Peter Motteux (Oxford, World's Classics), *1*, 6.
9. *Literary Relations of England and Germany in the Sixteenth Century*, p. 326.
Quoted by R. M. Alden, *The Rise of Formal Satire in England* (Philadelphia, 1899),
p. 15.

lusion. The allegorical satirist is more likely to achieve his purpose if he can sustain the attitude of the ironist who philosophically observes the incongruities of human life, for the reader makes the contradictory demands of detachment and guidance. The use of allegory enables the satirist to fulfill these conflicting requirements by giving a dramatic point of view to his disguised judgment.

It is impossible to consider the viewpoint of the judge without pondering the purpose for which the judgment is written. The consideration of purpose at once suggests another relation between satire and allegory, for the mainspring of both is the interplay of the general with the particular. Some larger truth is to be conveyed by the individual representation before us. Johnson in defining satire in the Dictionary declares: "Proper *satire* is distinguished, by the generality of the reflection, from a *lampoon* which is aimed against a particular person," and writers of satire have commonly disclaimed personal animus. Personal satire, to be sure, does exist; but its chances of survival are in exact proportion to the largeness of its application. If there were no modern Cibbers and Theobalds, *The Dunciad* would have fewer readers than it does; and it is safe to hazard the guess that there are fifty readers of *The Rape of the Lock* for one of *The Dunciad.* But it is the charm of the particulars quite as much as the persistent defects of society that makes the perennial delight of reading about Belinda and her lack of a sense of proportion. The same thing is true of allegory. We see ourselves and our friends in *Pilgrim's Progress;* but it is not just the fact that Mr. Worldly Wiseman and Talkative still exist, but the fact that Bunyan makes us see and hear them that keeps his allegory alive. They get expressed. When satire and allegory are vigorous and effective, both work in both directions: from the individual to his general characteristics and also in reverse order from larger truths to personal manifestation of them. The salutary interplay between abstract and concrete is indeed one source of the vigor we find in allegory and satire even when we do not find them in conjunction—as for instance in *The Divine Comedy* and *An Argument against Abolishing Christianity.* But the interplay is especially strong in allegorical satire. Sir Hudibras is vastly more entertaining than just any freakish knight would be because he epitomizes specific faults that Butler had observed in the Dissenters. His antics, on the other hand, give the very breath of energetic life to Butler's observations.

Achieving a just relation between the universal truth and the concrete fiction by which it is conveyed is a necessity common to satire and allegory. W. P. Ker speaks approvingly of reality's "breaking through and sweeping away the imagery"[1] in spiritual allegory; and we feel the appropriateness in fervid religious allegories like those of Dante and

1. "Allegory and Myth," *Collected Essays,* ed. Charles Whibley (London, 1925), *2,* 307.

Bunyan, whom he uses as examples, of the allegory's being sometimes swept aside for the direct presentation of truth. In allegory used for satire, however, the just relation seems to consist in sustaining a consciousness of both the allegorical representation and the truth being represented. Such double consciousness is essential if the allegory is to be maintained. This is not to suggest that every detail, especially in a long allegory like *Gulliver's Travels,* should bear a double meaning, but that the imagination of the reader should be kept steadily operating in two planes. If we use the allegory simply as a barrier to be leaped or a puzzle to be solved before we get to the meaning which is our object, we lose the very pleasure of indirection which is the basic delight that satire and allegory share. On the other hand, if we attend exclusively to the charm of the fable, we lose the point, the meaning which gives force and impetus to the allegorical representation. And likewise, if the satirist forgets one or the other, we feel that we have been unfairly dealt with, cheated of half our proper reward in reading him. Indeed the supreme satirists often sustain interest at more than two levels, as Swift does in giving, through little people who fascinate in their own right, his views not only on recent events in England and France but on human nature as well.

A further problem common to satire and allegory is the degree of similarity between the truth and its representation. If they converge, we lose the sense of metaphor altogether; if they are so remote that we are more conscious of antagonism than of likeness, we feel irritation rather than pleasure. The first difficulty is peculiarly that of the creator of satiric characters. If he is not skillful in adjusting representation to reality, he gives simply another version of the medieval pictures of the Seven Deadly Sins. Some of the 17th-century characters are lifeless for this reason; and there are few readers for Edward Young's *Love of Fame,* in spite of occasionally well-pointed couplets, because his Crassus, his Philander, his Narcissus, are distinguished hardly even in name from the abstractions they represent. That this difficulty in presenting figures who stand for qualities can be surmounted is brilliantly proved by Erasmus's delineation of Folly. The opposite difficulty of too great divergence has been especially the pitfall of the irresponsible satirists of the turn of the last century and after, whose fantasies sometimes seem to be pictures of nothing. Even *Erewhon* and *Erewhon Revisited,* with all their penetrating comment on English life, sometimes lapse into extravagance. The same conflict which engages contemporary critics about the degree of likeness which is desirable in metaphor in poetry applies to allegorical satire. The soundest conclusion seems to be that the satirist in allegory will seek a vehicle which has just enough incongruity to accentuate the likeness with which he is concerned. How much is enough, it is his artistic problem to determine in each case, remembering that both likeness and difference are useful. Reynard the Fox in the medieval beast epic the more reveals a kind of man for not being wholly man. In the hands of the successful artist the difference never leads to diffuseness. The satiric purpose is served by as much divergence as actually makes for economy.

Behind this effort to get the larger truth into particular and economical expression, there is usually a more compelling purpose on the part of both satirist and allegorist. This purpose can only be described as moral. Perhaps the most curious part of the remark of the critic who finds satire and allegory incompatible is his basing the incompatibility on the fact that allegory is didactic. No kind of writing is more frankly, sometimes blatantly, didactic than satire. In being used for instruction the two modes of writing have another affinity. The reader values the writer's concern for a standard of judgment and the reproof of defections from it, even though neither may hope for any actual reform. The air of detachment which we expect of the artist must not suggest for either allegorist or satirist a lack of concern, but rather a mastery of feeling. Earnestness is unseasonable only when it breaks the imaginative framework and so actually prevents expression. One of the distinctions between good and bad allegory, as between good and bad satire, is the degree of conviction which it carries. A quality that makes the reader turn in boredom from the more mechanical of the medieval allegories and from Marston's satires alike is the feeling that both were executed as set pieces or exercises on subjects about which the writer himself does not care very much.

The successful writer of both satire and allegory not only possesses a standard of judgment about which he cares, but he assumes that it is a just standard, accepted by right thinking people, who are his proper audience. And it is flattering to the reader to be considered part of that audience—fit, though few. If the writer's detachment implies superiority to the human foibles he depicts, it implies a like detachment on the part of the reader. In the same *Intelligencer III* in which he declares that he has "as good a title to laugh, as Men have to be ridiculous," Swift says that he wants to laugh "with a few friends in a corner." The sharing of the laughter intensifies the fun for the maker of the joke and his few friends alike by the extra pleasure of being in the special corner together. This situation of the reader's being taken into the writer's confidence applies equally to allegory. We do not identify ourselves with Phaedria as we read of her, but with Spenser in his condemnation of her. We are on his side, the "right" side. This power of allegory to put the reader in what the author regards as the proper point of view is one of the determining reasons why the satirist finds allegory so apt an instrument for his purpose. If we are to read either satire or allegory with pleasure, we must for the artistic moment at least have the point of view of the artist. His concern about his standard must be communicated; and we must share his angle of vision even when we are compelled to recognize the face in the

mirror as our own. This participation is the common source of the
artistic pleasure in allegory and satire and also the basis of their moral
effect.

Since there is so strong an affinity between satire and allegory, it is
reasonable to suppose that in satires projected as allegories, the excel-
lences and defects of the allegory will have a controlling effect upon the
success of the satire. Indeed the two must function as one. A work of
art is an organic unity; hence it is folly to judge an allegorical satire as if
the allegory were an extraneous interpolation. In so far as the work is
an imaginative whole, the allegory is the satire and the satire is the
allegory. This generalization holds throughout the variety of allegorical
structures used for satire. Among the common types of frameworks for
satiric allegories are stories of plot, the presentation of false heroes, animal
stories, journeys, and future worlds. To see how the satire operates as
allegory and the allegory as satire in some familiar examples of these
types will be the purpose of the following chapters.

2

Allegories Controlled by Plot

"a well-fram'd Tale handsomely told, as an agreeable Vehicle for Counsel or Reproof."

GEORGE FARQUHAR

NARRATIVE appears in most satiric allegories; and in a large group, it makes the predominant pattern of relationship. *Absalom and Achitophel* is one in which the ostensible object is the telling of a story where the action controls the conception. Thus, the shape of the narrative itself determines the structure of the piece and is responsible for the allegorical effect. The story is studded, to be sure, with the famous portraits of Achitophel and Zimri and the other participants in the political plot. Indeed, Sir Walter Scott excuses the abruptness with which the narrative breaks off by saying: "it may be considered as somewhat hard to expect the merit of a well-conducted story in a poem merely intended as a designation of various living characters. He who collects a gallery of portraits disclaims, by the very act of doing so, any intention of presenting a series of historical events." [1] But Dryden himself suggests that to present a series of historical events under the guise of retelling the Biblical narrative was exactly his intention; and his own explanation of why he "forbore to prosecute" the conclusion of the story is sound in literal fact as well as in the artistic framework of his allegorical scheme. When he says, "Were I the inventor, who am only the historian, I should certainly conclude the piece with the reconcilement of Absalom to David," [2] he is fitting events of 1681 precisely to the point at which he breaks off the Bible story. What distinguishes the poem as an allegorical satire is, in fact, "the merit of a well-conducted story" which Dryden achieves within the double confinement of a well-known Biblical narrative and still more familiar current events that must be fitted together without doing violence to either.

1. *John Dryden's Works,* ed. Sir Walter Scott and George Saintsbury (Edinburgh, 1882–93), 9, 203.
2. "To the Reader," *The Poetical Works of Dryden,* ed. George R. Noyes (Boston, 1950, Cambridge ed. of the Poets), p. 109. All quotations from the poems of Dryden are from this edition.

15

He starts off with all the zest of "once upon a time," removing the story into the enchanted world of make-believe and at the same time dealing tactfully with Charles II's promiscuity. The economy with which he projects the royal family situation while rousing anticipation is worthy of Chaucer. Then comes the gracefully turned picture of Absalom, with the relation between him and his father.

> What faults he had, (for who from faults is free?)
> His father could not, or he would not see.
>
> (ll. 35–6)

After this, before he gives the portrait of the next principal actor, Dryden packs the history of the Commonwealth and Restoration, with an analysis of the British temperament, "a headstrong, moody, murm'ring race," and an account of the Popish Plot, "Bad in itself, but represented worse," into a hundred brilliantly compressed lines. Enough praise has been lavished on the character of Achitophel as an evocation in a few lines of a complex being; but not enough has been made of how much the picture gains from the narrative background against which it is placed. Far from being a collection of portraits in a gallery, the characters of *Absalom and Achitophel* are actors in a dramatic story; and even when he comes to the lists of the supporters of both sides toward the end of the poem, Dryden not only gives vitality to the individuals portrayed, but disposes them in their proper places on the stage as leaders of the different parts of the troupe or mere extras, as their business in the action determines. Not for nothing had Dryden been turning out two plays a year for the delight of the court. He brings to bear in *Absalom and Achitophel* the feeling for structure and arrangement which is of the essence of the dramatist's, as of the storyteller's, art. When we reach the portrait of Achitophel, we have it intensified by the whole impression of uneasiness in the state, of the ferment of factions which has been described. Indeed, the opening line of the portrait announces Achitophel as the "first" of the "ungrateful men" who had been "rais'd in power and public office high."

Dryden shows his feeling for the structure of his allegory not just in the organization of the poem as a whole and in the disposition of the characters, but also in the management of individual scenes. The inherent drama of the temptation scene is brought out with the greatest finesse as he reveals the hesitation and the susceptibility to flattery of the youth and the guile of the tempter. He has already connected Achitophel with the father of all temptation, the devil; and now he adds the suggestion of devil as serpent:

> Him he attempts with studied arts to please,
> And sheds his venom in such words as these:
>
> (ll. 228–9)

We therefore bring to our feeling in the scene the intensification of awareness of the story of the Garden of Eden, and of Milton's treatment of that
archetype of all temptations. Dryden's procedure is strikingly like
Milton's, with which he has challenged comparison by announcing in the
preface: "But since the most excellent natures are always the most easy,
and, as being such, are the soonest perverted by ill counsels, especially
when baited with fame and glory; 'tis no more a wonder that he with-
stood not the temptations of Achitophel, than it was for Adam not to have
resisted the two devils, the serpent and the woman." Achitophel begins, as
does Satan, with flattery of a peculiarly seductive sort. Just as Satan tells
Eve that she should be adored as a goddess among numberless gods and
angels, so Achitophel asks Absalom:

> How long wilt thou the general joy detain,
> Starve, and defraud the people of thy reign?
>
> (ll. 244-5)

Like Eve, Absalom first rejects the suggested temptation:

> My father governs with unquestion'd right; . . .
> Mild, easy, humble, studious of our good;
>
> (ll. 317 and 325)

But again like Eve, Absalom shows his weakening under the stress of
flattery; and Achitophel, like his prototype, renews the attack:

> Him staggering so when hell's dire agent found,
> While fainting Virtue scarce maintain'd her ground,
> He pours fresh forces in, and thus replies.
>
> (ll. 373-5)

Achitophel even borrows two actual arguments from his father, the devil.
First, just as Satan accuses God of injustice, so Achitophel says:

> Would David have you thought his darling son?
> What means he then, to alienate the crown?
> The name of godly he may blush to bear;
> 'Tis after God's own heart to cheat his heir.
>
> (ll. 432-5)

Second, just as Satan suggests that God would really be pleased at the
boldness of Adam and Eve in eating the fruit, so Achitophel declares:

> He fears his brother, tho' he loves his son,
> For plighted vows too late to be undone.
> If so, by force he wishes to be gain'd;
> Like women's lechery to seem constrain'd.
> Doubt not: but, when he most affects the frown,
> Commit a pleasing rape upon the crown.
>
> (ll. 469-74)

But more impressive than particular parallels, is the power Dryden shares with Milton of arousing apprehension, of creating the feeling that the temptation is evil, that yielding to it will be disastrous, and at the same time of throwing by far the greater blame on the tempter. We fear for Absalom, as we do for Eve, though we know in each case that yielding to the temptation is sin. Thus the allegory intensifies the apprehension concerning Monmouth not just by presenting it in terms of Absalom, but also by suggesting echoes of the Garden of Eden. The whole scene is managed so as to create the true tragic qualm of concern for the actor who is about to bring ruin on himself and others by his own folly. Indeed, the entire narrative is conducted at that level of high comedy which is very close to tragedy.

Another manifestation of the elevation of tone is the formal speeches of Absalom and David which punctuate the action. Each one allegorizes exactly the points Dryden wishes to reveal at the same time that it intensifies the drama. Absalom's is a masterpiece of chicanery. His plea for the support of his countrymen appeals first to their pity for him as a person wronged, "a banish'd man," for their sakes, allegorizing exactly the arguments used in Monmouth's behalf. Then he appeals to national pride by saying that trade is falling and the Jebusites getting power. He makes, under the thinnest veil of filial respect, damning insinuations of his father's age and frivolousness, and ends with a tearful protestation of devotion to the people's cause. Dryden makes the speech serve Absalom's purpose well; but, what is more important, he makes it serve his own as artist. David's longer speech, which ends the poem, is deftly contrasted with Absalom's. It is marked throughout by quietness, dignity, authority. It conveys precisely the feeling Dryden intends, that here is a true statement of the case. Furthermore, it allegorizes the specific points Charles wanted made. Both speeches show Dryden to be the master of ratiocination that Johnson proclaimed him to be. Their discrimination from each other shows in addition how much he is also the master of the art of fitting speech to character to give verisimilitude to his allegory. The likeness and contrast between them is emphasized by their parallel placing in the narrative. Absalom's comes after the catalogue of his supporters, when a new movement is needed; and it makes the beginning of his action of displaying himself in public triumph while

> Fame runs before him as the morning star
> And shouts of joy salute him from afar.
>
> (ll. 733–4)

David's speech too comes after the catalogue of his supporters. But instead of inciting to action, it quells the insurrection. As the speech itself is marked by majestic calm instead of a demagogue's heroics, so the immediate result is altogether more solemn than Absalom's setting forth to dazzle the people. At the conclusion of David's speech, heaven ratifies what the king has said by the omen of thunder and the poem promptly, not to say abruptly, ends with the couplet:

> Once more the godlike David was restor'd,
> And willing nations knew their lawful lord.
>
> (ll. 1030–1)

These two set speeches are skillfully used in the structure of the poem to mark the two units of action, the acts, as it were, of the drama. At the same time they sharpen the impression of the two characters who speak them and are made more emphatic by coming from those characters. The emphasis which they thus both give to the structure and take from their position, and give to the characters and gain from being uttered by Absalom and David, means that they greatly intensify by their use in the allegory the point of the satire. Monmouth and Charles II hover close behind the figures in the poem.

From the beginning, Dryden has made his dramatically constructed story serve the purposes of allegory and satire. The surface narrative at once conceals and reveals its meaning. Dryden takes full advantage of the familiarity of the story he is using as a blind. Indeed he calls attention to the absence of novelty in the tale by choosing a story not only among the most familiar of Old Testament narratives, but also already connected with the current situation. Reference to Charles as David was a commonplace; and Achitophel was a usual term of opprobrium for a wicked politician. The prose tract called *Absalom's Conspiracy: or, the Tragedy of Treason,* which had appeared in 1680, sets forth the Bible story solemnly and with a good deal of effectiveness as a warning against foolish ambition. Dryden deliberately chooses a framework which is thoroughly known to his readers so as to give himself freedom to make his point about current affairs by intensifying the drama of the old story. Part of what enables him to do this so vigorously without ever seeming to go behind the imaginative front he has chosen as a disguise is that the framework of the blind is so well known that he can easily let the reader peer behind it for himself. We get at once the pleasure of being in the secret because Dryden supplies the clues to his real subject in the opening lines. But he never wavers from the pretense of telling a story of ancient times, so that throughout we have the specific allegorical enjoyment of being allowed to make the application independently. The indirection is perfectly sustained; and much of the aesthetic satisfaction comes from seeing how deftly the pieces of the familiar old story are fitted to the equally familiar current history. In the account of the commonwealth, for instance, when we read:

> They who, when Saul was dead, without a blow,
> Made foolish Ishbosheth the crown forego;

Who banish'd David did from Hebron bring,
And with a general shout proclaim'd him king;
(ll. 57–60)

we have the flattering sensation of having got the puzzle right ourselves;
and so we accept with more readiness the point that Dryden is making
about the fickle and headstrong people. In the same way when he comes
to the plot of Achitophel, we seem to be allowed to make the judgment,
though Dryden is guiding it by every device of narrative skill. This is
particularly true in the famous portraits. The men are described as actors
in the ostensible story and explained as types of human beings; but we
know who they really are and so derive a double pleasure from the acute-
ness of the portrait and the neatness with which it fits its subject.

How much Dryden gains from keeping alive the sense of the surface
story he seems to be telling is quickly demonstrated by comparing his
poem with any of the answers to it which mechanically use the same
allegorical scheme. The most familiar of these are Samuel Pordage's
Azaria and Hushai and Elkanah Settle's *Absalom Senior: or, Achitophel
Transpos'd.* In *Azaria and Hushai* whole speeches of characters are lifted
with very little change except in the name of the speaker. Thus Azaria,
who has Absalom's part, says:

Oh, would to Heaven I ne'er had been begot!
Or never had been born a Royal Blot!
(*Azaria and Hushai,* London, 1682, p. 19)

Of course Hushai, who is the Shaftesbury of the poem, is given the role of
wise counselor who restrains the natural ambition of the young prince;
but even so, he retains some of Achitophel's sharpness, advising:

Here you your Course must even steer and strait,
That you may not your Father's fears create;
Keep the *Jews* Love, and not increase his Hate.
(p. 21)

The description of the Jews, "a moody, murmuring, stubborn Race" is
largely copied from *Absalom and Achitophel.* These borrowings give
the poem some vitality; but Pordage does not succeed in fitting them into
a convincing narrative. They suggest the lion's skin on the form of the
ass. To make *Absalom Transpos'd,* Settle adopts a simpler system of
borrowing: as the title suggests, the characters are merely shifted, with
Shaftesbury turned into Barzillai, and more ludicrously, James, the
king's not much younger brother, into Absalom. Dryden's laughter at
Settle as Doeg understandably plays on the title of the poem when he
says:

> Instinct he follows, and no farther knows,
> For to write verse with him is to *transprose*.
> (*Absalom and Achitophel*, Pt. ii, ll. 443–4)

Nor is it any wonder that in the "Epistle to the Whigs" which precedes *The Medal* Dryden says: "If God has not blessed you with the talent of rhyming, make use of my poor stock and welcome." But so far as conveying the allegorical point is concerned, Settle's inability to handle a story and give it meaning is as much of a handicap as his lack of a talent for rhyming.

Even in *Absalom and Achitophel*, Part ii, the fiction is weak; and as Scott remarked, "there was little wit in continuing to draw out the allusion till it consisted in nothing more than the invention of a Jewish name for a British author or statesman, the attempt at finding prototypes in Scripture for every modern character being necessarily abandoned." [3] Tate, to be sure, lacked Dryden's power as a poet; but the continuation fails chiefly because it is weak as an allegorical story. The portraits of Og and Doeg, though they are executed by Dryden's hand at its most skillful, do not seize the imagination as do those of Achitophel and Zimri, who appear as actors in a vividly conceived narrative.

One of Dryden's most effective means of keeping alive the double consciousness on which allegory depends is the little aphoristic comments on human nature with which he points the moral of the seeming story. Since they are deliberately generalized, they compel attention beyond the action that has just been described. So the reader looks, as they suggest, at common human nature; but in so doing, he is reminded of the other particular application to which attention has already been directed. Thus the comments have a double allegorical impact.

> Plots, true or false, are necessary things,
> To raise up commonwealths, and ruin kings.
> (ll. 83–4)

The couplet fits what Dryden has been talking about in the outward story; but it also inevitably suggests not just universal history but the plots most recently in the minds of his readers in their own time and country. The statement:

> But when to sin our biass'd nature leans,
> The careful Devil is still at hand with means;
> (ll. 79–80)

perhaps the most famous couplet in the poem, operates in the same fashion. It is true of all mankind; but it is a comment on both the real and the fictitious action and marks a new movement in the story.

3. *Works*, ed. Scott and Saintsbury, *9*, 322.

The same sort of use is made of the comments on the actors. The couplet:

> So easy still it proves in factious times,
> With public zeal to cancel private crimes.
>
> (ll. 180–1)

fits Achitophel, about whom it purports to be said, and it is an apposite comment on a kind of scheming politician; but most of all, it points directly to Shaftesbury. The generalization:

> What cannot praise effect in mighty minds,
> When flattery soothes, and when ambition blinds!
>
> (ll. 303–4)

applies to the character of Absalom in the poem and at the same time tells us how Dryden wants us to think of Monmouth. The long passage of exposition in which Dryden develops the importance of a fixed succession is used in the same way.

> All other errors but disturb a state;
> But innovation is the blow of fate.
>
> (ll. 799–800)

The couplet gives the philosophy of government on which the whole narrative is based. It at once points the moral of the outward story and warns the English against following Monmouth.

Dryden has thus intensified the allegorical impact of his satire in a variety of ways. He has sharpened the interest by bringing out the inherent drama in the Biblical story and in its implications concerning the situation in England. He has sustained the two levels of interest all the way through by the skill with which he has pointed the parallels of character and parallels of action in the real and seeming stories. Finally, he has redoubled the allegorical force by giving aphoristic statement to the general truths which both surface and underlying story illustrate.

A Tale of a Tub is another satiric allegory in which, as the title declares, the story is the determining force. But Swift, instead of going to the Bible for the vehicle of his wit and playing upon the familiarity of the borrowed story as Dryden had done, chose (like the true modern who is supposed to be the author) to make a narrative from his own "Invention." [4] His choice is as sound for his purpose as Dryden's for his. The

---

4. See *A Tale of a Tub To which is added The Battle of the Books and the Mechanical Operation of the Spirit*, ed. A. C. Guthkelch and D. Nichol Smith (Oxford, 1920), pp. xxviii–xl for a treatment of various parallels to Swift's story. The narrative of the three rings is the nearest to Swift's assumed attitude of naïveté, but as the editors point

material which Swift wished to include is much broader in scope than Dryden's; and the adoption of a known story to carry it would have been a cramping restriction on the application of the point instead of an illumination of it. The relation of tenor and vehicle would necessarily have become forced and hence have made a barrier to quickness of comprehension and consequent aesthetic pleasure. Swift's material is immense in sweep: *"The Abuses in Religion he proposed to set forth in the Allegory of the Coats, and the three Brothers, which was to make up the Body of the Discourse. Those in Learning he chose to introduce by way of Digressions,"* as he explains in the "Apology." (p. 4) To fulfill such an intention, he needed to create his own story. Furthermore, the material which he wished to illumine by taking away the "Artifical *Mediums,* false Lights, refracted Angles, Varnish, and Tinsel" (p. 172) was not already in the public consciousness like the happenings of which Dryden treats. With the history of the church, Swift's audience was roughly familiar; but it was not a matter of immediate public moment like the episode in Dryden's poem. And the abuses in learning were attitudes rather than events. Whereas Dryden plays upon a sort of reciprocal familiarity of real and ostensible story, Swift is partly emphasizing how little known his real material is by making up a concocted story to carry it.

Swift's scheme differs from Dryden's not only in the creation of a new story for his allegory, but also in the organization of the whole. Whereas Dryden's construction is as tight as possible, Swift deliberately gives the impression of writings loosely thrown together. This impression of random discursiveness is an essential part of his mockery and is as deftly arranged and controlled as is Dryden's neatly managed plot.

The mind of his Modern, Swift meant to show up as confused; but he is far from being confused in his own mind as he creates it.[5] This "I" is as brilliantly conceived to serve Swift's allegorical purpose as is the "I" of *Gulliver's Travels*. He is immensely proud of being "the *freshest Modern*" (p. 130) and he has the true modern lack of reticence: "HAVING thus paid my due Deference and Acknowledgment to an establish'd Custom of our newest Authors, by a *long Digression unsought for,* and *an universal Censure unprovoked;* By forcing into the Light, with much Pains and Dexterity, my own Excellencies and other Mens Defaults, with great Justice to my self and Candor to them; I now happily resume my Subject, to the Infinite Satisfaction both of the Reader and the Author." (p. 132) In accordance with this sublime self-confidence, he is willing to help the less gifted: "Since my *Vein* is once opened, I am content to exhaust it all at a Running, for the peculiar Advantage of my dear Country,

out, the story itself actually bears little resemblance to Swift's. All references to *A Tale of a Tub* and *The Battle of the Books* are to this edition.

5. For a discussion of the role of the "I" see Robert C. Elliot, "Problems of Structure in *Tale of a Tub,*" *Publications of the Modern Language Association of America,* 66 (1951), 441–55.

and for the universal Benefit of Mankind." (p. 184) His stupidity is manifest in his every utterance. Yet this very stupidity, besides being in itself a devastating exposure of the modern pretenders to learning, gives Swift a chance to make ironic explanations of his intentions through the ingénu's naïve pronouncements: " 'TIS a great Ease to my Conscience that I have writ so elaborate and useful a Discourse without one grain of Satyr intermixt." (p. 48) At the same time, the ingénu's candor gives the impression that the surface story is true: "I shall by no means forget my Character of an Historian, to follow the Truth, step by step, whatever happens, or where-ever it may lead me." (p. 133) Such a mind is itself exactly suited to the childlike acceptance of the tale as given; and its point of view is communicated to us in spite of ourselves. The story begins with the fairy tale formula which assumes that the remote is to be taken as true; and with part of our consciousness at least, we take it in this way. The very simplicity of mind of Swift's instrument helps him to win from the reader a "willing suspension of disbelief."

But Swift does not intend to create complete poetic faith. The simple storyteller sometimes forgets himself and takes sides or becomes the Modern of the digressions. But the special device which Swift uses to undercut acceptance of the narrative is the notes, particularly those added in the fifth edition of 1710. The "I" who writes them is presumably the Bookseller, who has already revealed himself in "The Bookseller's Dedication to Lord Somers" to be thoroughly imbued with the same modern spirit which inspires the writer of the digressions. In the notes he stands off from the work he has in hand and makes comments, sometimes explanatory, sometimes derogatory, always proclaiming (as does his author, whom he resembles) that he has the true interest of the reader in mind. Like the author, he is willing to cream "off Nature" (p. 174) and tell what lies near the surface of his brain. Early in the story, he says helpfully, *It is likely the Author, in every one of these Changes in the Brother's Dresses, referrs to some particular Error in the* Church of Rome; *tho' it is not easy I think to apply them all."* (p. 86) He often confesses inability to understand his author, sometimes, in the best modern spirit, implying that this means the author is not worth understanding, but again suggesting that the mystery is especially profound. He comments on the digressions as well as on the surrounding story; and in a note on "A Digression on Madness" he suggests the true complexity of the implications: *"I cannot conjecture what the Author means here, or how this Chasm could be fill'd, tho' it is capable of more than one Interpretation."* (p. 179) It seems almost as if Swift himself is giving fair warning not to think that it is easy to exhaust his meaning.

The notes on the narrative have a curious double effect: while they interrupt the flow of the story and thus break in on acceptance of it, the apparent seriousness of the commentator beguiles the reader into taking

seriously what he is commenting on. This paradoxical effect of the notes
not only makes them peculiarly good fun in themselves, but also heightens
the paradoxical effect of the whole point of view of the work, which
superimposes layer upon layer in its complexity. One set of notes, added
in 1710, is taken over verbatim from Wotton's *Observations upon The
Tale of a Tub*. The words of the champion of the moderns are solemnly
inserted in the new edition of the Tale as the explanatory notes of "the
learned Commentator" (p. 73) and give still another facet to the mockery.

The digressions, like the notes, are part of the total metaphorical
framework. It is true that the allegory of the brothers and their coats is
distinct, as Swift himself declares in the Apology; but the whole piece is
allegorically conceived. Certainly in the digressions as truly as in the
Tale, Swift is saying one thing and intending something else; and certainly the pattern of relationship within the vehicle and the correspondence between vehicle and tenor are sustained. Each of the digressions is
a discourse which is to be read only by a special key: to take them as they
seem to be meant is to miss the point entirely. The Modern, as he stands
and preens himself before the world, praising himself for all the faults of
the moderns, is to be seen around and into quite as much as are Peter and
Jack in the Tale. In creating the digressions, Swift works somewhat as
does Erasmus when he lets Folly praise herself, though Swift's Modern
as he runs on displaying himself is allowed none of the charm of Erasmus's character as she rattles along about the various ways all men are
indebted to her. Swift does not intend to permit his reader a smile of
humorous sympathy in self-recognition. We are forbidden to feel self-
indulgent as we look beyond the mind of the ingénu speaker to Swift's
intent in such comments as:

> there is a peculiar *String* in the Harmony of Human Understanding,
> which in several individuals is exactly of the same Tuning. This, if you
> can dexterously screw up to its right Key, and then strike gently upon
> it; Whenever you have the Good Fortune to light among those of the
> same Pitch, they will by a secret necessary Sympathy, strike exactly
> at the same time. And in this one Circumstance, lies all the Skill or
> Luck of the Matter; for if you chance to jar the String among those
> who are either above or below your own Height, instead of subscribing
> to your Doctrine, they will tie you fast, call you Mad, and feed you with
> Bread and Water. (pp. 167–8)

While we wryly make the application of this analogy, the ingénu doubles
the force of the blow to our self-esteem by drawing the practical conclusion in terms of which most "philosophical" human beings live: "For,
to speak a bold Truth, it is a fatal Miscarriage, so ill to order Affairs, as
to pass for a *Fool* in one Company, when in another you might be treated
as a *Philosopher*." (p. 168) The helpful Modern leaves nothing unsaid.

His lack of restraint and Swift's lack of mercy, rip the veil from the human longing for approval even in the very digression that praises veils and identifies illusion with happiness. But to be happy is to be a fool: "This is the sublime and refined Point of Felicity, called, *the Possession of being well deceived;* The Serene Peaceful State of being a Fool among Knaves." (p. 174)

The Digression on Madness is not different in method, but only in intensity, from the other digressions. They uniformly communicate by means of sustained indirection. Furthermore, they are full, as the image of the harmony of strings illustrates, of little allegories. Swift's habit of imagination is both metaphorical and allegorical. The succession of metaphors for wisdom: a fox, a cheese, a sack-posset, a hen, a nut, does not have an allegorical effect. It is simply a string of images for the same idea, the difficulty of attaining wisdom and the disappointment in it once attained. But in the analysis of the views of those who "held the Universe to be a large *Suit of cloaths,* which *invests* every Thing" (p. 77), a whole pattern of relationship is consistently worked out within the one scheme, and the effect is truly allegorical. The force of the devastating paragraph about men as suits of clothes depends upon the structure of the whole small allegory. Indeed, Swift emphasizes this by the way he introduces the paragraph: "THESE *Postulata* being admitted, it will follow in due Course of Reasoning, that those Beings which the World calls improperly *Suits of Cloaths,* are in Reality the most refined Species of Animals, or to proceed higher, that they are Rational Creatures, or Men." (p. 78) Examples of both kinds of figures could be multiplied. The highly figurative quality of the style of both digressions and story sharpens particular meanings and is an intensification of the larger allegory by fostering an allegorical habit of response. It is thus an important means of enforcing the unity of the work.

In the story of the brothers and the coats, from which the supposed author constantly digresses, Swift reveals his mastery of the powers that make effective storytelling whether or not the story told is allegorical. First of all, his power of visualization is demonstrated in any number of vividly realized pictures. The chapter on Jack's frenzy, for instance, makes its point about his mind by giving the tatterdemalion physical existence from the collar stitched "so close, that it was ready to choak him, and squeezed out his Eyes at such a Rate, as one could see nothing but the White" (p. 199), to the "fluttering Appearance" of his rags, which by their "ridiculous Flanting" resemble Peter's finery. Throughout the Tale the reader is called upon to use his senses, especially that of sight, as the picture of Jack makes him do. The necessity of participation gives the story a peculiar vitality and contributes to the animation of the dramatic scenes and of the actors in them.

Since the characters are revealed in a series of episodes, the interest in action and the interest in people are gratified simultaneously. The brothers are constantly doing something, often something violent, and thus displaying themselves. Swift knows how to keep himself, and even his ingénu author, in the background. The story starts briskly with the father's deathbed injunction to his sons to mind their coats and proceeds at once to bring them up to town. Swift, like Fielding, announces that he will skip the blanks of history in which nothing exciting happens and so promises constant action, which immediately begins. The liveliness of the sentence that describes the brothers' improving "in the good Qualities of the Town" (p. 74) not only gives the feeling of their actual activities but by the way it runs on creates the impression of their busy rushing about in the attempt to become men of the world. Then after the account of the religion of clothes comes the scene of the brothers' finding authority for the decoration of their coats, though the literal-minded brother objects to accepting the prohibition against silver fringe as a prohibition against broomsticks, for the "Epithet, *Silver* . . . could not he humbly conceived, in Propriety of Speech be reasonably applied to a *Broom-stick.*" Then Swift laughs at the whole idea of allegory: "but it was replied upon him, that this Epithet was understood in a *Mythological,* and *Allegorical* Sense." (p. 88) It is a masterly little comic scene in itself; and, as Swift's allegories often do, carries two levels of implication beyond the outward story. It not only shows up the motives behind the accretions to the doctrine and practice of the early church; but even more it reveals the constant human trait of rationalization, the power to find reasons for what one wants to do. Swift drives home the application to all times by ironically insisting that his story takes place "in an Age so remote." (p. 81) It is worth noticing that all the brothers (hence all Christendom) are involved in this performance.

Section IV, which treats of the growing power and arrogance of the Church of Rome, continues the story of the brothers with equally vivid comedy. Again a long, lively list, with paragraphs on the purchase of a Continent in *Terra Australis incognita,* the Sovereign Remedy for Worms, the Whispering-Office, Ensurance, Universal Pickle, and Bulls, is followed by an episode in which the traits already suggested are conveyed dramatically. The homely vigor of Peter's bullying in the scene in which he tries to force the crust of a twelve-penny loaf on his brothers as flesh and wine is all too convincingly realistic. We hear actual people speaking in the most natural way in the most down to earth of domestic situations. The very tones of voice are registered and through them the petulance and timidity of the cowed brothers and the boisterous arrogance of Peter. Swift's ear was acute to catch the inflection of human speech. The same power to give the feeling of actually listening to talk which he shows in the *Polite Conversations,* almost his latest work, is already manifest here. It is the fact that he makes us really hear a dinner table squabble that

is shocking, for he also compels us to remember that the real subject is
Holy Communion, though as he says in the Apology, what he is mocking
is the "abuse" of transubstantiation. Like a good allegorist, he keeps alive
the awareness at once of tenor and vehicle; and it takes a strong palate to
relish the relation of this particular tenor to this particular vehicle. But
it is Swift's intention to shock in order to compel realization that the view
of the sacrament which Peter tries to impose is false. And as usual, he
links the particular meaning with a larger one. Ordinary bullies and their
victims who allow themselves to be imposed upon are mocked as much as
are Roman prelates and their dupes; and the larger satiric import lends
force to the particular satire. Yet all the time the story stays supposedly in
the realm of the three brothers. The chapter ends, as it has begun, without any confession that the author has a point of view at all, in vigorous
action. After Peter seems clearly mad, the younger brothers grow restive
and surreptitiously consult the father's will. This naturally starts inno-
vations, and "In the midst of all this Clutter and Revolution, in comes
Peter with a File of Dragoons at his Heels, and gathering from all Hands
what was in the Wind, He and his Gang, after several Millions of
Scurrilities and Curses, not very important here to repeat, by main Force,
very fairly kicks them both out of Doors, and would never let them
come under his Roof from that Day to this." (p. 122)

Section VI develops the differences between the two younger brothers:
"These two had lived in much Friendship and Agreement under the
Tyranny of their Brother *Peter,* as it is the Talent of Fellow-Sufferers
to do; Men in Misfortune, being like Men in the Dark, to whom all
Colours are the same: But when they came forward into the World, and
began to display themselves to each other, and to the Light, their Com-
plexions appear'd extremely different." (p. 134) In the vigorous scene
of the brothers' trying to rid their coats of excrescences, this difference
becomes very plain; and Swift first shows his contempt for Dissenters:
"For, (Courteous Reader) you are given to understand, that *Zeal* is never
so highly obliged, as when you set it a *Tearing:* and *Jack,* who doated on
that Quality in himself, allowed it at this time full Swinge." (p. 138)
So, in stripping off the gold lace, he tears his coat from top to bottom and
darns it with packthread and skewer; and in his rage over his difficulties
with the embroidery, he rips off the whole piece and flings it into the
kennel. Martin's remonstrances are unavailing: "In short, *Martin's
Patience* put *Jack* in a *Rage;* but that which most afflicted him was, to
observe his Brother's Coat so well reduced into a State of Innocence;
while his own was either wholly rent to his Shirt or those Places which
had scaped his cruel Clutches, were still in *Peter's* Livery." (p. 140)
Again the vehicle carries not just the comment on Presbyterians, but an
indictment of a common human trait—one that Swift never wearies of
trying to correct by showing it for what it is, whether the Moderns are

trying to level down the Ancients' peak of Parnassus to the height of their own, or the Lilliputians are wishing the Blefuscudian fleet wiped out. This episode ends with the highly pictorial account of Jack's running mad, which leads on to the discussion of the mad Aeolists and the Digression on Madness, and thence to the description of Jack's behavior when mad, which is really the end of the story. Like Dryden, Swift must end his narrative at the point reached by actual events; and since the Dissenters, in his view, are still running mad, he stops with the inconclusive conclusion, though he has not finished with the Dissenters and comes back to excoriate them in the *Mechanical Operation of the Spirit* after the lighter foolery of *The Battle of the Books*.

This survey of the dramatic episodes, undertaken to prove Swift's power to engage interest in action while revealing character, has also demonstrated the masterly organization of the story. Its clearness has always been simply taken for granted as an easy straight line running through what until recently seemed to critics like the welter of brilliant digressions.[6] It is true that the design of the narrative is simple in comparison with that of the digressions; but its simplicity is very carefully planned. Almost like the writer of a magazine serial, Swift gives in each section devoted to the story one movement of action (which bears exact correspondence to a unit of church history, to remember parenthetically the allegory in the serial) marked by one highly dramatic episode. Each time he breaks off for a digression at a point where interest is intensely engaged so that the reader is eager for the next installment. The interest is held over until the return to the story partly because the intervening material is not an interruption of idea, but an oblique comment on the narrative.

The clarity and suspense that mark the movement of the story are intensified by the pattern of arrangement of the three brothers with Martin in the middle. And again this arrangement is not an arbitrary device of the storyteller, but an integral part of Swift's point which the allegory is to carry. The main idea of the religious part of the work is that the Church of England is the church of the middle way and therefore the best. The parallel in the madness of Peter and Jack, with the greater extravagance in Jack's behavior, is not just a matter of structural design of repetition without reduplication: it makes the point that Swift wishes to make about Roman Catholicism and Presbyterianism and has the same distribution of emphasis on the aberrations of the two churches as does his nonallegorical *Sentiments of a Church of England Man*.

One part of his point Swift fails to get convincingly made in the allegory. Clearly he wishes Martin to seem the superior brother, and this

6. Miriam Starkman has shown in *Swift's Satire on Learning in A Tale of a Tub* (Princeton, 1950) how closely and with what subtle interrelations the digressions are actually linked to the surrounding tale.

he may be; but he is the least alive of the three. The failure to believe in
him may be due to the propensity of human nature to doubt goodness, for
as Fielding pointed out in *Tom Jones:* "Knavery and folly, though never
so exorbitant, will more easily meet with assent; for ill-nature adds great
support and strength to faith." Swift must bear the responsibility for part
of the difficulty, however, just as Fielding must for our not believing in
Squire Allworthy's perfections. The fallible characters are more vividly
presented by both authors. Just as we hear Squire Western hallooing and
see him capering about, so we hear Peter berating his brothers and see
the absurd spectacle Jack makes of himself as he stumbles blindly into
lamp posts or ditches. It seems to be true that Swift's sensory imagination, like Fielding's, worked more vigorously on a subject that he wished
to satirize than on one that he wished to praise. The characters from *A
Tale of a Tub* that are sharply etched on the consciousness are Peter and
Jack, not Martin; and the point that remains in the mind is about the
extremes of Roman Catholicism and dissent, not about the moderation of
the Church of England.

*A Full and True Account of the Battel Fought last Friday, between
the Antient and Modern Books in St. James's Library* is so closely connected with *A Tale of a Tub* that consideration of one leads directly to
consideration of the other; but the battle, although it too is dependent on
a narrative framework, uses a new kind of allegorical indirection. Swift's
"Account" is in mock heroic style; and the battle which is to show up the
absurdity of the whole quarrel between ancients and moderns is made
an imposing event. The inflation of the mock heroic manner gives a
special quality to any allegory; and it is a quality exactly suited to Swift's
satiric purpose here. He wishes, of course, to demonstrate the superiority
of the ancients, but even more to show the folly of the contestants in
engaging in the controversy. He adopts just the elaborate tone which will
emphasize the ridiculous in what he is mocking. Books of Controversy,
he announces before the battle begins, are "haunted by the most dis-
orderly Spirits." (p. 223) Although in a sense Swift is himself engaging
in the controversy, he does so in order to show that the solemn writings
which have preceded his are deplorable in spirit, that the whole quarrel
should never have been begun, and that having been begun, it should
have ended long ago:

> In this Quarrel, whole Rivulets of *Ink* have been exhausted, and the
> Virulence of both Parties enormously augmented. Now, it must here
> be understood, that *Ink* is the great missive Weapon, in all Battels of
> the *Learned,* which, convey'd thro' a sort of Engine, call'd a *Quill,* in-
> finite numbers of these are darted at the Enemy, by the Valiant on each

side, with equal Skill and Violence, as if it were an Engagement of
Porcupines. This malignant Liquor was compounded by the Engineer,
who invented it, of two Ingredients, which are *Gall* and *Copperas,* by
its Bitterness and Venom, to *Suit* in some degree, as well as to *Foment*
the Genius of the Combatants. (p. 221)

Swift's mockery of the bitterness in controversies of the learned is the
more effective because his own writing in this mock heroic extravaganza
is remarkably free of bitterness. He could write with more detached gaiety
about Bentley and Wotton than about the Dissenters; and the *Battel* is an
interval of fun before the scarifying unallegorical satire in the *Mechanical
Operation of the Spirit.*

The disclaimer in The Bookseller to the Reader sets the spirit of the
work: "I must warn the Reader, to beware of applying to Persons what
is here meant, only of Books in the most literal Sense. So, when *Virgil*
is mentioned, we are not to understand the Person of a famous Poet,
call'd by that Name, but only certain Sheets of Paper, bound up in
Leather, containing in Print, the Works of the said Poet, and so of the
rest." (p. 214) This air of not saying what he is saying is sustained and
governs the whole mock heroic management of the allegory. The Author's
Preface likewise helps to establish the tone: *"For, Anger and Fury,
though they add Strength to the* Sinews *of the* Body, *yet are found to
relax those of the* Mind, *and to render all its Efforts feeble and impotent."*
(p. 215) Throughout the work Swift never yields to anger and fury, and
the sinews of his mind are never relaxed.

His alertness is apparent in the arrangement of the whole as well as in
the management of the separate parts. The imposing introduction giving
the origin of war in an allegorical genealogy (War is the child of Pride,
which is related to "Beggary and Want," as in the case of the Moderns in
the present war) prepares with fitting mock solemnity for the central
allegory, with the account of the quarrel over the two peaks of Parnassus,
its incorporation in books of controversy, and the consequent battle of
the books. Once the battle is reached, there would seem little enough to
say about it; but Swift's ingenuity creates variety which compels interest
in the allegory itself and constantly sets its meaning in new lights. The
animated little apologue of the Spider and the Bee, which interrupts before the books actually engage each other, in its own fable and Aesop's
appropriate exposition of it, makes the point of the larger allegory explicit. When the tumult over Aesop's speech leads to fighting, Swift
stops again to give an account of the hosts engaged on each side. The
battle array is described in true epic fashion; and each descriptive phrase
conceals and reveals a judgment of the superiority of the ancients and the
absurdity of the moderns. Following the practice of Homer and Virgil,
Swift has the gods engage in the controversy and balances the visit of

Fame to the upper divinities by that of Momus to the den of Criticism. When the arrival of this repulsive deity gives the signal for the battle to begin, Swift recalls its object by engaging Aristotle with Bacon and Descartes, Virgil with Dryden, and Pindar with Cowley. But before the reader wearies of the matchings of ancients with parallel moderns, he introduces Bentley and Wotton, with the lively series of adventures of Bentley's stealing the armor of Aesop and Phalaris, Wotton's grazing Temple with his lance while Temple unaware continues to drink of Helicon, and Boyle's pursuit and capture of the two champions of the moderns. He calls this an Episode to justify the intrusion of human figures into the allegory; but their doings fit so naturally into the movement of the battle and so clearly make points beyond the outward action that there is no need of apology for their presence. For all its epic trappings, the whole work has an air of energy and dispatch. We are never allowed to grow bored with one kind of action before another is introduced. Guthkelch suggests that even the supposed lacunae in the manuscript "occur at points where the narrative is in danger of becoming monotonous—a thing very likely to happen in the description of a series of combats." [7]

Besides the balance and variation in the pattern of the action, another means which Swift uses to achieve the impression of liveliness in his surface story is the very epic devices which, if seriously used, would give weight and thickness of texture. And again the outer instruments, which are amusing in themselves, are kept constantly directed toward the inner targets, of which Swift never loses sight. Besides the mock solemn genealogies and allegories of abstractions like Pride and Fame and Criticism already mentioned, there are other incidental allegories such as that of the state of dogs quarreling over a bone. The epic similes make an even greater contribution to the spirit of the piece. They are among the most successful devices of ludicrous reduction, for the grandeur of the manner is totally belied by the homeliness of the comment:

> As when two *Mungrel-Curs,* whom *native Greediness,* and *domestick Want,* provoke, and join in Partnership, though fearful, nightly to invade the Folds of some rich Grazier; They with Tails depress'd, and lolling Tongues, creep soft and slow; mean while, the conscious *Moon* now in her *Zenith,* on their guilty Heads, darts perpendicular Rays; Nor dare they bark, though much provok'd at her refulgent Visage, whether seen in Puddle by Reflexion, or in Sphear direct; but one surveys the Region round, while t'other scouts the Plain, if haply, to discover at distance from the Flock, some *Carcass* half devoured, the Refuse of gorged Wolves, or ominous Ravens. (pp. 253–4)

Then comes the equally mock serious application of the picture to Bentley and Wotton: "So march'd this lovely, loving Pair of Friends." The other

7. *Battle of the Books,* ed. A. C. Guthkelch (King's Classics, London, 1908), p. 253.

animal similes are just as funny. The picture of a young lion who turns aside at the braying of a wild ass to portray Boyle's pursuit of Wotton is given in the most grandiose terms: "He vindicates the Honor of the Forest, and hunts the noisy, long-ear'd Animal." (p. 257) One of the most belittling comparisons is the concluding one, which begins by the authority of Homer with making the two champions of the moderns like an old woman's scattered geese, and ends with the transfixing of both Bentley and Wotton on Boyle's spear as a brace of woodcocks is trussed by a cook.

These similes are largely pictorial; and they are not the only pictures. As usual Swift makes the reader see what he is talking about with the body's as well as the mind's eye. Yet the physical picture seems always to enforce the mental one instead of obliterating it by a conflicting vividness. The account of the visit of the goddess Criticism to her son Wotton, which parodies that of Venus to Aeneas, pictures what happens:

> Having spoke thus, she took the ugliest of her Monsters, full glutted from her Spleen, and flung it invisibly into his Mouth; which flying strait up into his Head, squeez'd out his Eye-Balls, gave him a distorted Look, and half over-turned his Brain. Then she privately ordered two of her beloved Children, *Dulness* and *Ill-manners,* closely to attend his Person in all Encounters. Having thus accoutred him, she vanished in a Mist, and the *Hero* perceived it was the Goddess, his Mother. (p. 243)

The picture of Bentley with his armor "patch'd up of a thousand incoherent Pieces" (p. 251) and of Dryden with his helmet "nine times too large for the Head" (p. 247) and many others which are equally vivid all make a satiric point with neat appropriateness at the same time that they make the action graphic. What Swift conveys about Wotton's pertness in his answers to Temple, Bentley's collecting of other men's learning, and Dryden's inadequacy as a translator of Virgil is much more actually communicated than if he had said it directly. The figures that he depicts might almost be drawn to illustrate Addison's definition of the mock heroic in *Spectator, 249:* "Mean persons in the accoutrements of heroes." But they are not just exercises in ludicrous incongruity. They make the particular points that Swift wishes to make about the various writers and writings in the controversy that provoked the work; and, what is more important, they enable him to make his point about the habits of mind he is satirizing. As Guthkelch remarks: "In the matter of the *Epistles of Phalaris,* Temple and Swift were completely in the wrong; but . . . so far as Swift's book was a protest against pedantry it was on the right side." [8] It is the skill with which Swift allegorizes his protest in mock heroic narrative that gives it enduring interest.

8. Ibid., p. xliv.

3

Allegories of Mock Heroes

"for always the dulness of the fool is the whetstone of the wits."
SHAKESPEARE

FOOLS abound in the satiric narratives just considered; but the story is the chief instrument in conveying the point. Indeed, in the discussion of the "mirth and gaiety" of Varronian satire in "A Discourse concerning the Original and Progress of Satire" prefixed to his translations of Juvenal, Dryden, by his treatment of the usefulness of narrative to Varronian satirists from Petronius to himself, seems to make narrative a criterion of the type. Thus he often employs a feigned story to carry his satiric meaning. There are allegorical satires, however, where the hero, or antihero, dominates the action which, if it exists at all, exists only to display his folly. Dryden's own *Mac Flecknoe* is such a satire, one in which the shape of the narrative is determined by the adventures of a mock hero. Its affinity in structure is with *Hudibras,* where the character is in control, rather than with *Absalom and Achitophel* and *A Tale of a Tub,* where the action prefigures actual events and therefore in a measure predetermines the behavior of the actors. The story which simply follows the adventures of a mock hero leaves the writer complete freedom of invention and yet gives him a narrative framework in which to operate. In *Mac Flecknoe* Dryden has used his freedom to create just the narrative situation which, now that he has invented it, seems the inevitable one in terms of which to make his point.

His objects are twofold: to annihilate Shadwell and to demolish literary stupidity itself. The scheme of having Shadwell succeed to the throne of Dulness enables him not only to accomplish both purposes, but to make them serve each other, for especially in the speeches of Flecknoe in praise of his son, Dryden can define the very essence of Nonsense without letting the old monarch for a moment lose character. The doubleness of perception, the seeing through what Flecknoe says into what Dryden means, is what constitutes the special pleasure of reading the poem and makes it give the authentic allegorical elation of seeing into a concealed meaning.

34

Since the narrative concerns so grand an episode as succession to a throne, Dryden properly assumes a mock solemn tone from which he never wavers. The sententiousness of the first four lines might almost be serious, except for the mention of Flecknoe's name. But the next couplet:

> In prose and verse, was own'd without dispute
> Thro' all the realms of *Nonsense* absolute.

(ll. 5–6)

without any wavering of the dignity of the music, precipitates the mirth that has been lurking in the first lines; and from there on the reader knows that the real meaning is behind the ostensible one. The impression of the long and peaceful reign of Flecknoe, and his "issue of a large increase" with its implication of the ubiquity of fools, leads straight to the waging of "immortal war with wit," and creates both dismay at the thing represented and delight at the representation. With the injection of Shadwell's name near the beginning of Flecknoe's first speech comes still another level of meaning with consequent intensification of effect. Here as hero is a real fool, or at least a real man whom Dryden, however justly or unjustly, chooses to call a fool. He gives vitality to the principles of folly enunciated by the aged monarch, at the same time that he receives meaning by exemplifying the essence of natural stupidity, "Mature in dulness from his tender years." Very early in the poem Dryden makes clear the concentration of his attack upon literary folly by having Flecknoe, still meditating the succession, speak of earlier dramatists as types of Shadwell, the "last great prophet of tautology."

The use of allusions to Shadwell's plays is deft throughout the poem; but they are all linked to ideas about writing itself and all woven into the fabric of the episode. The lines:

> St. André's feet ne'er kept more equal time,
> Not ev'n the feet of thy own *Psyche's* rhyme;

(ll. 53–4)

let the flat, mechanical verse of Shadwell's opera, for which the French dancer had been brought to London, carry the condemnation of all dull poetizing. The praise, "So just, so like tautology, they fell," makes the satiric point with fine irony, though it stays completely within the allegorical conception. In the descriptive passage, sharp in direct sense impressions and even sharper in implications, after Flecknoe has finished speaking, there is the same relating of Shadwell to others who "wage harmless war with words." He it is who is "Born for a scourge of wit, and flail of sense"; and in proof of this Dryden packs references to six of Shadwell's plays into the next four lines. But still the allegorical method is preserved. The phrase "scatter'd limbs of mangled poets" gives a vivid picture which compels the mind to go beyond it to the satiric point.

The description of the hero is perfectly in keeping with his father's account of his character:

> His brows thick fogs, instead of glories, grace,
> And lambent dulness play'd around his face.
>
> (ll. 110–11)

The omens of ale and poppies and owls all enforce the impression of the outward scene and yet have their special appropriateness of suggestion. The oath, "Ne'er to have peace with wit, nor truce with sense," keeps up the burlesque of a coronation scene, but reminds the reader inexorably of the endless fight against sense and of Shadwell's particular continuation of it.

Flecknoe's final address is the most delicate interweaving in the whole poem of the faults of bad writers: impudence, ignorance, "fruitless industry," "want of sense," "false flowers of rhetoric," labored dulness, creeping numbers, with references to Shadwell's own bad writing. The allusions: "hungry *Epsom* prose," "Sir Formal's oratory will be thine," "northern dedications," "let no alien S-dl-y interpose," "thou whole Eth'rege dost transfuse to thine," "arrogating Jonson's hostile name," recall the particular plays *Epsom Wells* and *The Virtuoso,* in which Sir Formal spouts his stream of speech, the fulsome dedications of Shadwell's plays to the Duke of Newcastle, his literary thefts from Sedley and Etherege, and his constant boasts of writing the drama of humors as a follower of Ben Jonson. But they do more than recall particulars; they continue the impression of what bad writing is and link Shadwell's actual writings with the essence of literary folly. The peroration of the speech, the urgent advice:

> Leave writing plays, and choose for thy command
> Some peaceful province in acrostic land.
> There thou may'st wings display, and altars raise,
> And torture one poor word ten thousand ways.
>
> (ll. 205–8)

perfectly completes the linking of the particular writer with bad writing in general and perfectly winds up the allegorical scene of the old monarch's speech making.

After this, when nothing remains that can improve the episode, Dryden borrows a bit of farce from one of Shadwell's own plays and has two characters from *The Virtuoso* who had played the same trick on Sir Formal, drop the "yet declaiming bard" through a trap door, while

> The mantle fell to the young prophet's part,
> With double portion of his father's art.
>
> (ll. 216–17)

As a bit of allegorical action, perfectly incorporating the point of the story, this ending is hardly surpassed by the yawn of Dulness at the end of *The Dunciad*.

The whole episode conforms to the standard for allegory laid down in the preface to *The Country-mouse and the City-mouse* in which Montague and Prior mock *The Hind and the Panther* for not keeping to its allegorical frame: *"All their Fables carry a double meaning; the Story is one and intire; the Characters the same throughout, not broken or chang'd, and always conformable to the Nature of the Creatures they introduce."* [1] Whatever the faults of *The Hind and the Panther* as allegory, in *Mac Flecknoe* Dryden shows that with another sort of material and with a wholly satiric intention, he can concoct an allegorical episode that gives his true meaning with just the right degree of veiling, and that he can sustain the little drama with "the story . . . one and intire; the characters the same throughout." His skill as an allegorist has much to do with his skill as a satirist.

Hudibras is a longer example of a Varronian satire in Dryden's sense of the term and of a satire of a mock hero. It is a freely constructed narrative, full of "mirth and gaiety" in which the person ridiculed is principal actor. What shape it has comes from the adventures of the supposed hero. It is also like Dryden's satires in being allegorical in method. Hudibras and Ralph are very much themselves, but also obviously very much more than themselves. They are so much more, in fact, that it has been impossible to attach them to particular historical figures, though the game of identifying individuals in the poem has exercised such fascination for scholars that their investigation of it has largely been an exploring of possible models for Butler's characters. Literary critics, on the other hand, have been so bewitched by the brilliance of the couplets that one even suggests discarding the bulk of the poem in order to display its units,[2] feeling apparently that the whole is less than the sum of its parts. But *Hudibras* rewards consideration in its total structure as satiric allegory. Such a consideration throws light on the virtues and defects of the poem which have been fairly consistently pointed out at least since Johnson's Life of Butler. Furthermore, it can reasonably be suggested that such a treatment conforms to Butler's own view of *Hudibras*.

Butler's pondering over the use of allegory is repeatedly revealed in his *Characters* and "Miscellaneous Observations." The wide scattering of his comments makes them the more emphatic testimony to his preoccu-

1. *The Hind and the Panther, transvers'd To the Story of the Country-Mouse and the City-Mouse* (1687), A₃–A₃ᵛ.

2. Edmund Blunden, "Some Remarks on *Hudibras*," *London Mercury, 18* (1928), 172–7.

pation with the purpose of indirection in art. He says concerning Books and Authors:

> Men take so much Delight in lying that Truth is sometimes forcd to disguise herself in the habit of Falshood to get entertainment as in Fables and Apologues frequently usd by the Ancients, and in this she is not at all unjust, for Falshood do's very commonly usurp her Person.[3]

In discoursing of Reason, he has already projected the same view of fiction:

> Betweene this [Falshood], and Truth, ly's the Proper Sphere of wit, which though it seeme to incline to falshood, do's it only to give Intelligence to Truth. For as there is a Trick in Arithmetique, By giving a False Number, to finde out a True one: So wit by a certaine slight of the Minde, deliver's things otherwise than they are in Nature, by rendring them greater or lesse then they really are (which is cal'd Hyperbole) or by putting them into some other condition then Nature ever did . . . But when it imploys those things which it borrows of Falshood, to the Benefit and advantage of Truth, as in Allegories, Fables, and Apologues, it is of excellent use, as making a Deeper impression into the mindes of Men then if the same Truths were plainely deliver'd. So likewise it becomes as pernicious, when it take's that from Truth which it use's in the service of Error and Falshood; as when it wrest's things from their right meaning to a sense that was never intended.[4]

He clings to the old conception of fiction as falsehood in a comment in which, though he thrusts it into the character of A Player in a thoroughly offhand manner, he seems almost to define for himself the province of the art of representation:

> It is not strange that the world is so delighted with fiction, and so averse to truth, since the mere imitation of a thing is more pleasant than the thing it self, as a good picture of a bad face is a better object than the face itself.[5]

The inadequacy, even the perversity, of human reason, which forms the basis of Butler's view of the purpose of fable, is succinctly put in his Observations on Books and Authors:

3. "Miscellaneous Observations and Reflections on Various Subjects," *Characters and Passages from Note-books,* ed. A. R. Waller (Cambridge, 1908), p. 401.
4. "Miscellaneous Observations," p. 336.
5. *Characters,* p. 249.

He that would write obscure to the People neede's write nothing but plaine Reason, and Sense, then which Nothing can be more Mysterious to them. *For to whom Mysterious things are plaine, plain Things must be mysterious.*[6]

The same human predilection for the lie is expressed in *Hudibras* itself:

> The World is nat'rally averse
> To all the Truth, it sees or hears
> But swallows Nonsense, and a Lie,
> With Greediness and Gluttony.
> (III. ii. 805–8) [7]

Butler is clearcut and implacable about the moral function of allegory:

> Allegories are only usefull when they serve as Instances, to illustrate Some obscure Truth: But when a Truth, Plaine enough, is forcd to serve an Allegory, it is a proepostorous mistake of the end of it; which is to make obscure things Plaine, not Plaine things obscure; and is *no less foolish, then if wee should looke upon things that ly before us with a Perspective, which is so far from assisting the sight, that it utterly obstructs it* beside the Prepostorous Difficulty of forcing things against their Naturall inclinations, which at the best do's but discover how much wit a man may have to no purpose; there being no such Argument of a slight minde as an elaborate Triffle.[8]

His conception of the moral purpose of satire is just as clear in a little conceit which is itself an allegorical satire in small:

> A Satyr is a kinde of Knight Errant that goe's upon Adventures, to Relieve the Distressed Damsel Virtue, and Redeeme Honor out of Inchanted Castles, And opprest Truth, and Reason out of the Captivity of Gyants or Magitians: and though his meaning be very honest, yet some believe he is no wiser then those wandring Heros usd to be, though his Performances and Atchievements be ever so Renownd and Heroicall. And as those worthys if they Livd in our Days, would hardly be able to Defend themselves against the Laws against vagabonds, So our modern Satyr has enough to do to secure himselfe against the Penaltys of Scandalum Magnatum, and Libells.[9]

It is hard to believe that in such comments Butler does not have his own principal work in mind. At any rate, he is shaping the conception of allegorical satire by which it is written.

6. "Miscellaneous Observations," p. 397.

7. Quotations are from Zachary Grey's edition (London, 1744) because it gives line numbers, as A. R. Waller's (Cambridge, 1905) does not.

8. "Miscellaneous Observations," p. 397.

9. *Characters*, Appendix, p. 469.

Since the object of his mockery was to be the misuse of the mind, all the extravagances of unreason,[1] Butler chose the strongest illustration available to him in the religious bickerings of the mid-century. In the quarrels of the Saints he saw demonstrated the faults that most repelled him: argumentativeness, and a manipulation of reason for the rationalization of false arguments, together with a setting aside of reason to trust individual, irrational manifestations of so-called truth. Combined with and accentuating these defects of intellect were those of spirit: avarice as a motive, self-righteous arrogance, hypocrisy, and dishonor regarding oaths. Such was Butler's view of the Puritans as it is directly set forth in one biting portrait after another in his *Characters.* The characters and miscellaneous writings not only clarify the habit of mind and total philosophic attitude manifest in *Hudibras,* but even depict with straightforward scorn the very traits Butler is ridiculing in the poem. Philosophically they are illuminating as to the basic ideas, the fundamental judgments, in terms of which *Hudibras* is conceived. Furthermore, A Quarreler, An Obstinate Man, An Hypocrite, and many more give positive help in interpreting particular characters in the poem. But artistically they are even more illuminating in a negative way, for they are written without the help of any fiction; and sharp as their directness is, they do not take hold of the imagination as the poem does. Because of the allegorical representation, *Hudibras* makes "a Deeper impression into the mindes of Men then if the same Truths were plainely deliver'd." The *Characters* portray the same people, observed by the same keen, skeptical intelligence; but we see the truth more clearly in *Hudibras* because, in keeping with his artistic theory, Butler is there giving it the help of a lie. In the *Characters,* for all his definiteness, Butler is dealing with types, and even the descriptions of his contemporaries remain general: the characters of A Fifth-Monarchy Man and An Anabaptist owe something to that of A Fanatic. The sharpness of the criticism comes from the positive set of values in terms of which Butler is viewing persistent defections from it.

In *Hudibras* the standard of values is the same. So is the choice of illustrations, though its range is more limited, for in the *Characters,* Roman Catholics draw as much of Butler's fire as do Dissenters, whereas the poem concentrates on Presbyterians, Independents, and other sectaries. But there is still the feeling that Butler is saying something about constant human traits, though he now presents them in terms of particular human beings. The "Late Wars" afford the amplest illustrations of the points he wants to make. In the poem, however, instead of writing

1. Cf. Ricardo Quintana, "John Hall of Durham and Samuel Butler: A Note," *Modern Language Notes, 44* (1929), 176–9; and "Samuel Butler: A Restoration Figure in a Modern Light," *A Journal of English Literary History, 18* (1951), 7–31.

directly about contemporary types, he uses the wit which "by a certaine slight of Minde, deliver's things otherwise then they are in Nature." *Hudibras* is a convincing demonstration of the claim he makes for such imaginative indirection: that "it is of excellent use, as making a Deeper impression into the mindes of Men then if the same Truths were plainely deliver'd."

By choosing to couch his satire in allegory, he creates for himself the problems of conceiving appropriate fictional characters to embody his meaning and of involving them in appropriate action to sustain his point. Of all the varieties of fable open to Butler, he chooses perhaps the most difficult: simply a set of adventures of a mock hero in a real world. He gives himself none of the help of the writer of animal allegory or the creator of fantastic worlds, for whom the levels of the apparent story and the real story are so obviously distinct that once he leads the reader into making the initial adjustment, he can write almost straightforwardly and trust that the vehicle and the tenor of the allegory will be grasped almost simultaneously. Butler's characters, while they may be freaks, are still human beings; and their actions, while they may be fantastic, must be possible for human beings. Yet their distinctness from the world of fact must be preserved. The proximity of the planes of reality and representation is what makes the neatness and the difficulty of the problem. The world in which the creatures of Butler's imagination function is the English world in which bear baitings and skimmingtons and the rogueries of astrologers and lawyers actually took place. The world of the surface narrative is part of the same world which Presbyterians and Independents would inhabit if they were being portrayed directly. Thus in both character and action, Butler is dealing with the familiar and the actual, simply out of focus. It is a peculiarly complicated mode of indirection which he employs, a peculiarly intellectual one, involving constant adjustments of judgment as well as of imagination. Butler is not wholly successful in sustaining it; but it is a brilliant choice of imaginative framework for what he wishes to communicate. Hudibras is a burlesque, a caricature of a proper human being, just as the traits which he represents are in reality distortions of the proper mind of man. The actions in which he is involved are fantastic, just as the behavior of real people in its baseness and irrationality is a travesty of behavior appropriate to man.

In order to establish the impression of Hudibras, Butler gives first a survey of the confusion of his mental traits. His stoutness is mentioned early; but it is not until his oddities of mind have been thoroughly reviewed that there is any extended description of his person. This makes the object of Butler's satire unmistakably clear in the very beginning; and it is also unmistakable that the method of condemnation is mockery through distortion, not straightforward analysis and reproof. Each trait in turn is held up to the refracting mirror of Butler's mind. Hudibras is "shy of using" his wit; he displays tags of learning inappropriately; he corrupts logic to split hairs; he uses geometry for measuring food and drink; by divination he can tell:

> Whether the Serpent, at the fall
> Had cloven Feet, or none at all;
>   (I. i. 183–4)

he proves his religion by contentiousness. The couplet:

> A Sect, whose chief Devotion lies
> In odd perverse Antipathies,
>   (I. i. 207–8)

might be taken as the summary of his mind. Perversity in the use of his powers, misapplication of what talents he has, make him already a caricature of a person. So far Hudibras might be one of the *Characters,* or a combination of An Hypocritical Nonconformist and An Hermetic Philosopher. Only after establishing the impression of his temperament does Butler make use of physical description. The oddity of the knight's mind has prepared for the craziness of his appearance. Butler is reversing the common practice of the satiric allegorist of alluring the imagination first through sense impressions. But the use of physical detail when it does come is deft. Butler uses it to complete the winning of poetic faith in his knight as hero of a fictitious action rather than of a character essay. Once we have seen the knight's beard, with its upper part of whey and its "nether orange mixed with grey" as a "hairy meteor," we are convinced of his artistic existence. But the physical is the enforcement of the mental image. Hudibras wears his beard unshorn until the king shall be overthrown; and such a bizarre use of his beard fits the description of his mind. Butler proceeds in exactly the same way in the description of his figure. He barely pauses to show the hunched back and huge paunch of Hudibras before he uses the size of the paunch as a point of departure to speak of the gluttony of his hero, a subject which is continued in the description of his breeches. Such physical details as there are, are all extravagant; but they simply enforce the impression of the mind "perverse and opposite." The knight's physical actions, too, come now as the expression and accompaniment of a mind already known as ridiculous. The lack of physical coordination suggests that of mental motions:

> But first with nimble active Force
> He got on th' Outside of his *Horse,*
> For having but one Stirrup ty'd
> T'his Saddle, on the further Side,

> It was so short, h'had much ado
> To reach it with his desp'rate Toe.
> But after many Strains and Heaves,
> He got up to the Saddle-Eaves.
> From whence he vaulted into th'Seat,
> With so much Vigour, Strength and Heat,
> That he had almost tumbled over
> With his own Weight, but did recover,
> By laying hold on Tail and Main;
> Which oft he us'd instead of Rein.
>
> (1. i. 405–18)

It is impossible to see this picture of bodily awkwardness without feeling that it betokens mental absurdity. At least it is impossible to do so reading it in context, for the first strong conviction of the absurdity of the mind of the knight is still in control. This impression is sustained whenever Butler uses physical representation. Oddly enough, it is only when Hudibras speaks, as he does repeatedly and at length, that we occasionally lose the impression. But when we see him falling on the Bear, or running from the skimmington, or picking Sidrophel's pockets, we are convinced that he is part knave and part the tool "that Knaves do work with, call'd a Fool."

In the description of Ralph, the procedure is curious. There is not a single detail of his appearance; what is being mocked is first the low social status of the Independents and second their pretension to "Gifts" and "New-light." But there is such a wealth of physical detail in the imagery that we have the impression of seeing Ralph as a figure and reaching his significance allegorically. The cross-legged knights that give at once an image of Templars and of tailors, the

> *Dark-Lanthorn* of the Spirit,
> Which none see by but those that bear it:
>
> (1. i. 505–6)

with its property of leading men to dip themselves in dirty ponds, and playing upon "The Nose of Saint, like Bag-pipe Drone": all this wealth of sense impression gives us the feeling of seeing Ralph, when actually all we have seen is his mind, ignorant and misled by fancied inspiration. The same method of creating illusion is followed in presenting Sidrophel, Whachum, and the widow.

The company of grotesques who make up the bear-baiting group are much more briefly dealt with; but the procedure is similar. A quarrel-some crew is to be presented; and the few physical details sharpen the impression of pugnacity and suggest the people who make up the group: Crowdero is most completely described with his warped ear, grisly beard, and leg of oak; Orsin is stout, but the description concentrates on his stoutness of mind, and more space is given to his pouch of quack medicines than to his person; Bruin's visage is formidably grim; Trulla is simply a lusty virago; the treatment of Talgol is taken up with a mock heroic presentation of his exploits of butchering cows and sheep, that of Magnano with the same sort of suggestion of his tinker's calling, and the one of Cordon with references to his cobbler's trade; and finally Colon, the hostler, is presented in terms of equestrian feats. The object is simply to present them as a group of low combatants; and the few tumultuous details vigorously convey the physical, and hence the intellectual, impression of an angry crowd. Hardin Craig's identification of them as Parliamentary leaders is ingenious [2] and not out of keeping with Butler's own comment:

> [I] am content (since I cannot helpe it) y^t everyman should make what applications he pleases of it, either to himselfe or others, Butt I Assure you my cheife designe was onely to give ye world a Just Acco^t of ye Ridiculous folly & Knavery of ye Presbiterian & Independent Factions then in power.[3]

However the antagonists of Hudibras and Ralph are particularly identified, the point of the bickering among dissenting groups is roundly made; and the hilarious rough and tumble of the fight is perfectly suited to these common folk, whether Butler means the extra implication to be a slur upon the lowly origins of the upstart sectaries or a slur upon the temper of mind that makes important people act like hoodlums. Their coarse violence is exposed and through it the contentiousness of the Puritans and of man. The episode is one of the funniest low comedy scenes in the poem. The quality of the actors, the kind of action, and the mocking point to be made, all concur to produce the desired effect. It is a perfect little allegorical satire in itself with its point completely digested into the imaginative scheme and yet completely made.

Hudibras himself is steadily absurd in his behavior as the figure in the outward action; and the overweening, dictatorial temper of the Presbyterians, and of a certain sort of human beings, is never far from consciousness during his performance. Though the way Hudibras conducts himself is ludicrous, it is not without courage. Indeed, he often displays a reckless daring, what Butler calls a "high, outrageous Mettle," from his first rant, preaching peace among the Saints by surveying their past combativeness, to his last misguided blow against Trulla. Johnson charges Butler with unfairly making Hudibras a coward: "If Hudibras be considered

---

2. Hardin Craig, "Hudibras and the Politics of 1647," *Manly Anniversary Studies* (Chicago, 1925), pp. 145–55.

3. Quoted by Ricardo Quintana, "Butler-Oxenden Correspondence," *Modern Language Notes, 48* (1933), 4.

as the representative of the presbyterians it is not easy to say why his weapons should be represented as ridiculous or useless, for, whatever judgement might be passed upon their knowledge or their arguments, experience had sufficiently shewn that their swords were not to be despised." [4] To be sure, the pistol of Hudibras is made ridiculous:

> But *Pallas* came in Shape of Rust,
> And 'twixt the Spring and Hammer thrust
> Her *Gorgon* Shield.
>
> (I. ii. 782–4)

But it is possible that the fact that

> his Toledo trusty
> For want of fighting was grown rusty
> (I. i. 359–60)

signifies no more than that there had been a period of peace before the civil wars broke out. Hudibras comes off victorious in the first battle; and the shot he lets fly at random in the second does considerable damage. It is true that he is afraid at the approach of the skimmington which creates the center of action in Part II; but he rebukes the procession as boldly as he had done the bear baiters. In Canto iii of Part II he attacks Sidrophel with violence, though he does flee, supposedly leaving Ralph to take the blame when he thinks Sidrophel dead. He is afraid to give himself the whipping penance prescribed by the widow and is full of fear of the devils' drubbing he receives at her house. Yet Butler does not make him wholly a coward. His alternations of fear and rash boldness show the perversity and inconsistency which is his only consistency. Butler uses the fear which makes him betray his promise to the widow and his flight from her house as opportunities for the mordantly satiric passages of rationalization about the setting aside of oaths and of the mock philosophy of war ending with the description of Caligula:

> That triumph'd o'er the *British* Sea
> Took Crabs and Oysters Prisoners,
> And Lobsters, 'stead of Cuirasiers;
> Engag'd his Legions in fierce Bustles,
> With Periwinkles, Prawns, and Muscles;
> And led his Troops with furious Gallops,
> To charge whole Regiments of Scallops;
> Not like their ancient Way of War,
> To wait on his triumphal Carr:
> But when he went to dine or sup,

4. Samuel Johnson, *Lives of the English Poets,* ed. G. B. Hill (Oxford, 1905), *I,* 210.

> More bravely eat his Captives up;
> And left all War, by his Example,
> Reduc'd to vict'ling of a Camp well.
>> (III. iii. 360–72)

Hudibras is rather irrational and hypocritical than cowardly.

But the question of Butler's fairness in his portrayal, which Johnson's objection raises, is important, for the impression of fairness is essential to the success of a satiric portrait. A modern critic of Butler begins a section entitled "Faults and abuses of the time imputed to Puritanism" by saying: "Yet many other things are ridiculed in Hudibras which had nothing to do with Puritanism, but which Butler ridicules in the doings and sayings of the Presbyterian Knight. This is of course not quite fair even in an author whose set aim is ridicule, burlesque, satire." [5] Butler is accused of mocking Presbyterians as believers in astrology and witchcraft; but actually Hudibras has little faith in astrology. He is hostile to Sidrophel, and his whole conversation with him is an expression of disbelief. It is Ralph who urges consulting the astrologer, saying:

> Do not our great *Reformers* use
> This *Sidrophel* to forbode *News*.
>> (II. iii. 171–2)

Certainly William Lilly, who was at least one of the models for Sidrophel, was consulted by Parliament; and belief in witchcraft did exist among the Puritans, as Hopkins, the notorious witch hunter, demonstrates. It is further objected that Butler attributes licentiousness to the Puritans. Yet in point of morality, what Butler is mocking is clearly not their special immorality, but their claim to sainthood, the sins which *"Saints* have title to."

> For *Saints* may do the same Things by
> The *Spirit*, in Sincerity,
> Which other Men are tempted to,
> And at the devil's Instance do.
>> (II. ii. 235–8)

In any case, the love story of Hudibras is a story of the love of wealth. Cupid takes his stand "upon a Widow's Jointure land." Hudibras is perfectly frank about this:

> Let me your Fortune but possess,
> And settle your Person how you please.
>> (II. i. 477–8)

5. J. Veldkamp, *Samuel Butler, the Author of Hudibras* (Amsterdam, 1923), p. 101. The section continues to p. 113.

The lady is equally candid:

> 'Tis not those *Orient Pearls,* our Teeth
> That you are so transported with;
> But those we wear about our Necks,
> Produce those amorous Effects.
> Nor is't those *Threads* of *Gold,* our *Hair,*
> The *Perriwigs you make us wear;*
> But those bright *Guineas* in our Chests
> That light the wild-fire in your Breasts.
> ("The Lady's Answer," ll. 65–72)

The avarice of the knight is what Butler is ridiculing. There is another charge against Butler that he satirizes "the perverted chivalry of the time . . . in the person of 'the Presbyter Knight.'" Chivalry, however, is not one of the objects of satire at all, but an external part of the scheme for presenting the satire. Butler is not writing another *Don Quixote,* but merely using Cervantes' scheme of action to give a framework for his allegory. The perverted chivalry of Hudibras is part of the disguise, the falsehood, which Butler is using to present his truth. To consider this part of the device for conveying the point as being itself one of the objects of satire is in so far to miss the sense of the fiction. The very obviousness with which Butler thrusts references to Romance into the narrative, as for instance at the beginning of Part I, Canto ii, suggests that he feels the need of a reminder that he has employed the terms of chivalry for his framework. The accusation of injustice in particular points of satire can be dismissed by appeal to the poem itself.

But the comparison with Cervantes suggests the whole question of attitude toward the hero; and on this score the fairness of Butler may be challenged. The impression of unfairness is rather an aesthetic than a moral defect in the poem. Butler's artistic point of view is perfectly consistent: it is an angle of vision that creates steady distortion and persistently reveals the perverted human mind that he scorns. But it is exactly his unmitigated scorn which prevents the final success of his point of view. The reader is likely to share Johnson's feeling: "But for poor Hudibras, his poet had no tenderness; he chuses not that any pity should be shewn or respect paid him: he gives him up at once to laughter and contempt, without any quality that can dignify or protect him." [6] Butler has fallen into the difficulty inherent in the kind of representation he has chosen. If distortion is his medium, consistency of distortion should be a virtue, but the excess of the virtue here makes a defect. The portrait is so full of vitality that it sweeps the reader along; but if it leaves him artistically disturbed rather than satisfied, the reason for uneasiness may lie

6. *Lives of the English Poets, I,* 210.

partly in Butler's excess of zeal in heaping opprobrium on his victim.
What is important is not whether the Presbyterians had each particular
folly displayed by Hudibras, but whether he is a satisfying symbol of
human extravagance of mind. His not quite being so is what keeps him
from supreme allegorical fitness. We cannot entirely relate the vehicle to
the tenor, the knight to what he stands for. The portrait seems over-
drawn so that the reception of Hudibras as an artistic creation is inter-
fered with by the question of whether the human mind is as distempered
as is this image of it.

Though probability, once "certain suppositions" [7] have been made, is
the important artistic consideration, the questions just raised lead to the
constantly teasing one of whether the characters are also allegorical representations of persons who actually existed. Grey in the preface to his
edition makes it part of his praise "that the greatest part of the Poem
contains a *Series* of Adventures that did really happen: all the real Persons shadow'd under fictitious Characters will be brought to view from
Sir *Roger L'Estrange, who* being personally acquainted with the *Poet,*
undoubtedly received the Secret from him." The key attributed to
L'Estrange was published with Butler's *Posthumous Works* in 1715;
and perhaps the game of identifying the actors in Butler's drama had begun before that, as there being a demand for a key would imply. Scholars
in our own century suggest keys quite different from that of L'Estrange;
but controversies over the particular model for a particular fictitious character ignore the natural supposition that more than one actual man contributed to the making of Hudibras or Sidrophel or Whachum. It is perfectly conceivable, and indeed in keeping with the mode of composition
suggested by his commonplace books, that Butler noted traits from a
great number of sources and then put them together as they suited his
purposes. The characters are dramatized representations of general types
that may be drawn from as wide a variety of sources as the pictures of A
Modern Politician and A Dunce in the *Characters.* It is possible, and
indeed likely, that Butler's intention is to make them stand only for
habits of mind as do the inhabitants of Brobdingnag, rather than for
individuals as do Flimnap and Reldresal and other figures in Lilliput. In
any case, it is their vitality in displaying persistent follies which gives
them their enduring interest. The excitement of linking them with particular people who did live in history comes from the fact that they do
live in art, not the other way around.

The other part of Grey's sentence, "that the greatest part of the Poem
contains a *Series* of Adventures that did really happen," suggests a consideration of the action in which the characters are involved. Grey seems
to mean no more than that bear baitings, for instance, did take place and
were subjects of controversy. Such praise seems curiously misplaced.

7. Ibid., p. 216.

Literal realism, where it exists at all, is obviously the least of Butler's concerns. Just as we know from the beginning that the knight is more than a knight, so we know that his adventures are more than attempts to stop a bear baiting and a skimmington, more than courtship of a widow and consultation with an astrologer and a lawyer. But again, as in judging the characters, we wonder if the episodes prefigure actual events or simply a kind of event that the civil wars had made familiar. Butler's own statement: "Butt I Assure you my cheife designe was onely to give ye world a Just Acco^t of ye Ridiculous folly & Knavery of ye Presbiterian & Independent Factions then in power," is of no help, for he could have given a just account using either sort of allegorical representation. It is a temptation to see particular historical events in the episodes; but any close analogy breaks down. The most ingenious suggestions of scholars present difficulties. Any attempt to make the events of the story yield up their secret compels the conclusion that they simply have nothing to conceal in specific historical event. What they hold is the "Truth in Person" like "Words congeal'd in Northern Air"; but it is a truth about the kind of mad action Butler had witnessed during the period of the wars, not about the particular events of those wars.

For Butler's purpose this was a sound choice. It fits the conception of his characters, who are absurdly distorted actors representing absurd distortions of human intellect as especially manifest in "the Late Wars." The action in which they are involved is appropriate to them in the mode in which they exist. These grotesques are engaged in grotesque adventures. For Hudibras to have eggs thrown at his beard and devils pummel him fits the world of fantastic horseplay that he inhabits. A comparison with Book I of *Gulliver* emphasizes Butler's wisdom. Since Swift is using a realistic mode with reduction of size as the only means of sharpening the effect of the Lilliputians as human beings, he can best make his point by involving them in adventures that exactly parallel real historical events, letting the absurdity of the small people come out in the pettiness of their actions. But since Butler's artistic mode is distortion, he would have to distort history to fit a scheme of exact correspondence and precisely in so doing would make the exact correspondence break down. Furthermore, the wars were already a travesty of what history should be. The artist can better represent this general travesty by using farcical travesty of human actions of individuals for his allegory than by making a one-to-one equation of his metaphorical action with particular events.

The organization of the poem has often been criticized for lack of connection between the episodes. But Butler forestalls this objection by choosing the framework of romance for his allegory. The adventures are all the adventures of the same mock hero except the straight historical drama in Part III, Canto ii, which is frankly a digression. *Hudibras* is as unified as is *Don Quixote,* from which its scheme of organization comes, or as the picaresque novels with which it has inherent affinity.

A more important artistic consideration is whether the loose structure is allegorically sound. To this test it measures up admirably. Butler suggests that confusion and inconsequence of events are the inevitable result of the unsound principles of the participants in the events. The attempt to suppress the bear baiting and the love of the widow's jointure, which are juxtaposed in the poem, have no more to do with each other than have rigid, domineering self-righteousness and avarice, which are juxtaposed in the mind of the Puritan as Butler conceived him. The odd, perverse antipathies of the protagonists produce the inconsequence of the action.

If, then, the action is allegorically right in the buffoonery of the episodes and right in the randomness of the structure, what are its faults? There are two important ones. The poem is too long. However much we should like to know what further action Butler had in mind for his hero, we cannot really wish *Hudibras* longer than it is. A more serious defect is linked with the first. Part of the length of the poem is due to the length of the conversations. Much of the best wit is contained in the speeches of the characters so that it would be rash to wish them away; but they do not get wholly digested into the allegorical framework and so make a confusion of artistic effect. The conversation between Hudibras and Ralph in the first canto seems perfectly in character and in keeping with the metaphorical scheme that has been established. The jargon of Privilege, Fundamental Laws, thorough Reformation, etc., with which Ralph's speech is larded seems just part of his distorted view of bear baiting, and a legitimate reminder of what is being mocked. The conversation purports to be a discussion of bear baiting per se and gives its further meaning entirely allegorically. But with the harangue of Hudibras to the rabble, the poem moves into a different imaginative mode. Butler is giving the history of actual events from 1638 to 1643. The old covenant, the Bishops' Wars, the et cetera oath, the Six Members quarrel, the Solemn League and Covenant, and making war for the king against himself, are all used as arguments to break up the bear baiting, the controversy over which must now be linked with these actual historical events as a quarrel among the Saints. The only indirection in the rant of Hudibras is that Butler's own scorn of the Puritans is steadily revealed to the reader through Hudibras's honorific survey of their actions. The speech is extremely funny in itself and very pointed satire. But it departs from the allegorical world which has been projected by the representations before it and which reappears when the characters begin to act. From that point on, one is never sure in which world the characters are going to speak. Ralph congratulates Hudibras after the first encounter as a self-denying conqueror; and we wonder for a moment if we have been concerned with the battle of Naseby. The rest of Ralph's speech is much better digested into the allegorical framework. His talk of revelation and

Perfection-Truths has no special reference, it fits his character, which is altogether more consistent than that of Hudibras, and it is a perfectly possible comment from such a person on the situation in the poem. But after the second round of the battle when Ralph and Hudibras are in the stocks, Butler again moves from the sphere of allegorical representation of the foolish controversies of the Saints to direct discussion of them. Again the shift is suddenly made. Hudibras, like the absurd knight originally presented, is comforting himself with ends of verse and philosophical tags, bolstering his self-esteem by saying:

> If he, that in the Field is slain,
> Be in the *Bed of Honour* lain;
> He that is beaten may be sed
> To lie in Honour's *Truckle-Bed*.
> (1. iii. 1047–50)

when Ralph speaks directly of Presbyterian zeal and wit; and from there on the quarrel is about synods as "mystical Bear-Gardens." Again it is extremely clever satire in itself and succeeds in making both Presbyterians and Independents ridiculous. The gallimaufry of terms in Ralph's speech: Gospel-Light, Dispensations, Gifts, Grace, Spiritual Calling, Regeneration, and a dozen more, make skillful mockery of the vocabulary which seemed to Butler pure cant. But the debate over *"Synods* or *Bears"* repeatedly jerks the reader back and forth between the two modes of conception.

In Part II some of the speeches have the same effect. The harangue of Hudibras to the skimmington crowd, like that to the bear baiters, deals with straight history: the support of women to the Cause. The discussions of Hudibras and Ralph on breaking oaths and on going to Sidrophel since Saints may do what they please, present without allegory what Butler took to be Puritan attitudes. The discussion of oaths is perhaps the most mordant satire in the poem; but it is full of references to actual history which fit confusedly with the issue of whether Hudibras can swear with impunity that he has received the whipping and with the horseplay at the end when he attempts to give Ralph the whipping as his proxy.

The point of view in the poem is further confused by the fact that the conversations with the widow and with the lawyer are kept entirely away from history. The mockery of motive in them is general and is completely wrought into the story of the knight as such. On the other hand, in the second canto of Part III, after the section of narrative of historical events (which seems almost the straight telling of what has already been allegorically presented), come two speeches which are supposedly really uttered in the Rump, not in the imagined world of Hudibras and Ralph at all.

Therefore the feeling that there is unwarranted confusion in the poem comes not from disorganization in the action, which fits the total conception, but from the shifts in focus in the speeches from allegory to straight satire and back again. Thus the consideration of the poem as allegory throws light on the prevailing feeling among literary critics that it is a collection of brilliant sections rather than a coherent work of art.

The presentation of character is a central part of the art of the allegorical satirist. In *Hudibras* and *Mac Flecknoe,* the very titles declare the importance of the mock heroes whose adventures the poems relate. Nevertheless, it is through their adventures that they are known. The poems exist as narratives revealing the characters of their protagonists. The question arises whether there is such a creation as an allegorical character per se, or whether an allegorical character is simply a character who acts in an allegorical fiction and cannot exist without the surrounding story. Dryden's account of Varronian satire seems to make a story the necessary vehicle of the "mirth and gaiety." The usefulness of narrative to Dryden himself in presenting satiric characters is demonstrated not just in *Mac Flecknoe,* where the character evolves throughout the action, but in the force which the distinct portraits in *Absalom and Achitophel* gain from the story in which they are set. Nevertheless, the "characters" of *Absalom and Achitophel* can be read detached from the action. Within the pattern of the narrative, they clearly have an allegorical function; but if they are read alone, it is not clear that they are inherently allegorical. Pope's Atticus, to choose one out of the array of his satiric characters, exists in a carefully created artistic situation, but not in a narrative; and we do not think of the portrait as allegorical. Such characters appeal to the imagination as satiric distillations of the traits of certain sorts of people, and usually of individuals as well, but they are hardly allegorical except in the shifting of the name of the character. The satiric character which relates the individual to the type has a representational quality; but a consideration of the character tradition shows that the representation is not allegorical.

It is a great temptation to the critic interested in satiric allegorical characters to look for them in the immense body of Theophrastan characters. In the *Characters* of Theophrastus himself, we start off with "Garrulity is the delivering of talk that is irrelevant, or long and unconsidered," or "Parsimony is a neglect of honour when it involves expense"; [8] but at once we are involved in the chatter of the garrulous man or the actions of the parsimonious man. They are set forth with such keenly observed objective detail that the impression is of seeing actual

8. *The Characters of Theophrastus,* tr. J. M. Edmonds (Loeb Classics, 1929), pp. 47, 97.

men acting in a characteristic way, though only one trait is displayed. The Flatterer, the Newsmaker, and the Coward stand simply for themselves, however, and for all men like them in the particular quality revealed, not for something other than themselves. The intensification comes from a heightening of identity rather than from the pointing out of likeness within difference. The representation does not have the specific allegorical quality of standing for something other than itself. Indeed, Benjamin Boyce seems to use the term "allegorical figures" to exclude some of Dekker's sketches from the class of true characters; and he is disparaging the characters of Breton when he calls their subject "a personified abstraction, not an abstracted person." His definition of the form is clarifying: "The Character at its best—in Theophrastus or the Overbury collection or John Earle—is a highly artificial form. It is lively, yet basically it is neither dialogue nor drama; it represents a class, yet it must seem to possess the reality of a flesh-and-blood individual; it pleases by graphic detail and illumines by hints, yet it must not be endangered by the merely local and temporary." [9] By this criterion, we must reluctantly reject as nonallegorical the whole delightfully satiric array of characters, not only those who fall within Boyce's scope, but even their later progeny such as Ned Softly and Tom Folio and Lady Bustle and Beau Tibbs. They are more than themselves in what they represent, but not other than themselves.

Since the character as a form must be given up as allegorical, the question remains whether a satiric allegorical figure can exist without an allegorical story, whether such a narrative as *Mac Flecknoe* or *Hudibras* is the only way of presenting allegorically the foolish traits of men. Certain medieval representations of the Seven Deadly Sins seem to detach the figures from any plot. The realistically sketched Sinners in *Piers Plowman* are bound together only by the act of confession; but they are hardly allegorical. Surely the most striking presentation of an allegorical figure existing without an allegorical story is Erasmus's portrayal of Folly, the speaker in *The Praise of Folly*. She has no action whatever. She only speaks, and that within the set rhetorical framework of the classical oration. But she has, or seems to have, what she calls "the chief solace of life, uninhibited garrulousness" [1] so that by the end of the speech she is completely revealed. She has an existence of her own, quite apart from that of the foolish men she talks about as her beneficiaries. She is a vivid, variable, complex personality, always essentially herself. Yet she always represents something other than herself, to wit, human foolishness.

It is not difficult to show her distinctness from the trait she represents. First of all, she is completely feminine. She insistently reminds the audi-

9. Benjamin Boyce, *The Theophrastan Character in England to 1642* (Cambridge, Mass., 1947), pp. 211, 192, and 19.
1. Tr. H. H. Hudson (Princeton, 1941), p. 18. All references are to this edition.

ence that she is a "woman—a stupid animal, God wot, and a giddy one,
yet funny and sweet—so that in domestic familiarity her folly might
leaven the lumpishness of the male temperament." (p. 23) Her final
apology is: "If anything I have said shall seem too saucy or too glib, stop
and think: 'tis Folly, and a woman, that has spoken." (p. 125) Yet most
of the company of the initiates of Folly whom she surveys are masculine:
grammarians, monks, philosophers, lawyers, theologians—all men yield
to her sway. Much of the charm of the book comes from the charm of this
giddy lady whom the bachelor Erasmus with his masculine vision makes
convincingly funny and appealing in all her humanly contradictory traits
and views, a completely individual character.

She is captivating from the moment she steps up and begins to talk
about the cheering effect she has on gods and men. She is herself unfailingly and chattily cheerful in manner whether she is talking about the
boons she confers on men or about the oddity of the fact that while all
men follow her, none has yet praised her. We hear almost the tone of voice
of the good-hearted, garrulous woman as she pauses to say, "my breath is
giving out" (p. 11) or "I have just now been able to dig him up." (p. 32)
Her complacency is imperturbable, for she has the happiest origin, the
widest sway, and the most beneficent effects upon her devotees of any of
the divinities. She is puzzled over the ingratitude men show in failing to
sacrifice to her or build temples in her honor; but she comfortably declares: "Yet in my easy-going way I take this in good part, though I
could scarcely complain, with any grace, about the lack of such attentions;
for why should I demand incense or meal or a he-goat or a she-hog, when
men in all parts of the world unanimously accord me that kind of worship which is specially approved by our divines? Maybe I ought to envy
Diana, because she is appeased by human blood! No, I consider that I
am most piously worshipped when men—and they all do it—take me to
their souls, manifest me in their actions, and represent me in their lives."
(p. 66) In return, her helpfulness to her votaries is boundless, for she
makes possible friendship, marriage, and civil society. She can give both
pleasure and fortune; and the people with the closest affinity to her—
children, dotards, natural fools, and amiable madmen—are the happiest.

She pokes a good deal of obvious fun, as when she laughs at the
rhetoricians "who believe themselves absolutely to be gods if they can
show themselves bilingual (like a horse-leech)" (pp. 10–11) or the
lawyers who "equipped with three syllogisms" (p. 76) join battle on any
subject, or when she says of the philosopher, "Invite him to a ball, and
you learn how a camel dances." (p. 33) But more often, her approval is
Erasmus's poking fun. The essence of her character is Erasmian irony;
and what gives her her compelling human fascination is that it is often impossible to say with absolute assurance (except as her own votary) when
she is an ingénue disguise whom Erasmus intends to be interpreted by

opposites, and when he approves of her good sense. Part of the proof that all readers are in their degrees under her dominion is that all will be likely to decide independently where she is indeed speaking foolishly and where speaking truth with the license of a fool. What she says of self-love seems sheer good sense: "For what is so foolish as to be satisfied with yourself? Or to admire yourself? Yet on the other hand, if you are displeased with yourself, what can you do that is pleasing or graceful or seemly?" (p. 29) Her comment on the value of illusion has all the penetration of Swift's Digression on Madness without Swift's harshness. Her account of her making bearable the ills of life, especially old age, also has Swift's insight without Swift's bitterness. Her picture of the miseries of old age has much in common with the picture of the Struldbrugs; but her old men are not miserable because she has endowed them with her own spirit of folly. These pretenders to youth seem foolish indeed. But why are they more foolish than the acceptors of disguise? The praise of folly in war seems clearly ironic; yet there is a double edge even here, for "is not war the seed-plot and fountain of renowned actions?" (p. 30) Among the most fruitful ambiguities are those in the sections where Erasmus lets Folly mock at his own professions of philosophy and scholarship. The whole picture of those "who write learnedly for the verdict of a few scholars" is extravagantly humorous; yet anyone who inhabits the haunts of scholars must recognize the picture, perhaps even of himself:

> they add, they alter, they blot something out, they put it back in, they do their work over, they recast it, they show it to their friends, they keep it for nine years; yet they never satisfy themselves. At such a rate they buy an empty reward, namely, praise—and that the praise of a handful. They buy it with such an expense of long hours, so much loss of that sweetest of all things, sleep, so much sweat, so many vexations. Add also the loss of health, the wreck of their good looks, weakness of eyes or even blindness, poverty, malice, denial of pleasures, premature old age, and early death—and if there are other things like these, add them. The scholar considers himself compensated for such ills when he wins the approbation of one or two other weak-eyed scholars. (pp. 73–4)

As so often happens with the best satire, there is a basis of sympathetic affection in Erasmus's laughter. Perhaps Folly's own gift of self-love is in operation.

Certainly Folly is not identical with these scholars, nor with any of the others of the hosts of fools over whom she holds sway. She retains her allegorical distinctness. She is the cause of men's foolish actions, not the doer of them in her own person. Indeed, it is only after her own temperament has been thoroughly established that Erasmus presents the array of fools: merchants, grammarians, poets, authors, lawyers, logicians, sophists, scientists, theologians, monks, kings, courtiers, bishops, cardinals, popes, and priests. The section describing them is the longest in the whole oration, for Folly embraces all men in her "provident goodness." (p. 65) The descriptions of the various kinds of fools are almost like Theophrastan characters and are etched with their own distinctness; they are not to be confused with Folly. She retains her separate character as she describes her votaries. These sketches in themselves are done with far more art than those in *The Ship of Folys* or the *Steele Glas;* but one compelling reason for the far greater charm of Erasmus's book than of other collections of fools is the central character of Folly, the allegorical figure, essentially herself, yet giving always a notion of something other than herself.

In fact she remains more steadily allegorical than satirical. In the last sections of her speech where she is talking of the folly of religion, she is voicing some of Erasmus's profoundest spiritual insights. The paradox of Christianity itself is the final one expressed by this paradoxical creature; but in the very end, she reverts to her earlier gaiety and finishes her brief apology: "And so farewell. . . . Applaud . . . live . . . drink . . . O most distinguished initiates of Folly!"

4

Animal Stories

"prettie Allegories stealing under the formall Tales of beastes, makes many more beastly then beastes: begin to heare the sound of vertue from these dumb speakers."

SIR PHILIP SIDNEY

BRUTE creation seems sometimes to exist as a satire on mankind. All that the allegorist needs to do is to point the parallel. Moralists have used man's likeness to the animals for instruction in a variety of ways ranging from the strange edification of the medieval bestiary to the reproof of the newspaper political cartoon. There has never been a time when men were not trying to teach each other the lessons to be learned from the creatures. The Bible is full of such teaching; and the stories spread under the name of Aesop are probably more widely known than any other classical literature. The Orient is as rich as the Occident in this lore; and the African folk tales, many of which reappear with a new set of animal characters in the Uncle Remus stories, attest the vitality of the genre without dependence on a written language.

Sometimes the teaching is so explicit that the resulting work cannot be called allegory. This is true of many of the fables of Aesop and his successors; but it is a significant proof of the value of indirection in art, even the art of pedagogy, that the best and best known of the Aesopic fables label the moral and leave it as something distinct and outside the story instead of making it explicit within the narrative. The ones that do point the lesson within the tale are the least effective of the group. When the mother of the wayward thrush explains to her son, who wants to make a companion of the swallow, that friendship between those who cannot bear the same climate is folly, we have the feeling that the bird would have learned more by making the experiment and we by watching its outcome. In this fable, the moral is at least dramatized to the extent of being explained to a character within the action. The reader is even more dismayed when the point is simply explained directly to him, as in the fable of Jupiter's not granting horns to the camel because the prayer was for something nature had not intended. The more artistic fables tell the story and stop like true allegories, allowing the reader the pleasure of drawing his own conclusion before he reaches the labeled moral, which remains outside the story.

When the cock tells the fox who has been preaching a general peace among the animals in order to make the cock come down out of the tree, that the dogs are coming, the story is complete with the dramatic ending of the fox's running off. When the fox who has refused to visit the sick lion says that he notices tracks of other animals going to the lion's palace, but none coming away, we know what to think without having the moral further pointed. The moral is left suspended within the tale in all the most familiar of Aesop's fables: The Fox and the Grapes, The Dog in the Manger, The Hare and the Tortoise, The Fox and the Stork, The Dog and His Shadow, and the Country Mouse and the City Mouse. And when any of these reappear in the writings of sophisticated artists, as when Horace retells the last named story, the same rule holds. The artist respects the integrity of the story and the intelligence of the reader and lets the tale make its own point. Perhaps L'Estrange is right in the preface to his edition of the Fables when he says that we are all like children and prefer the pill of moral teaching sweetened with the pleasure of the tale.[1] Nor do we want the pleasure of the allegory spoiled by being told that it is really moral medicine after all. The moral labeled and separated from the tale as is customary in Aesop's stories, we accept without protest because no disguise is presented, and there is therefore no violation of conception; but having the moral stated within the story, where we expect to get it only through the images, destroys the imaginative effect which it has been the whole object of the story to produce. The case is somewhat altered in a work like Swift's "Beasts' Confession," where the application is longer than the tale, and the animal allegory serves just as introduction to the classes of mankind who mistake their talents. But even here Swift announces the pointing of the moral as distinct from the tale.

A different sort of problem is created by the animal story which is instruction about man observed from the point of view of the animals. A highly effective example of this use of the beasts is Johnson's *Idler, 22* [2] in which the old vulture gives instruction to her young about the order of the universe in which man is created as the "natural food of a vulture." The mother bird, in response to the puzzled inquiry as to how man is to be killed if he is so much bigger and stronger than the vulture, replies:

> "We have not the strength of man . . . and I am sometimes in doubt whether we have the subtilty; and the vultures would seldom feast upon his flesh, had not nature, that devoted him to our uses, infused into

1. *Fables of Aesop and Other Eminent Mythologists: with Morals and Reflexions* by *Sir Roger L'Estrange* (London, 1692), A₂.

2. Johnson omitted this essay from collected editions of the *Idler;* but it is reprinted at the end of Chalmers's edition. The quotations are from *British Essayists*, ed. A. Chalmers (Boston, 1864), *27,* 400–2.

him a strange ferocity, which I have never observed in any other being that feeds upon the earth. Two herds of men will often meet and
shake the earth with noise, and fill the air with fire. When you hear
noise, and see fire, with flashes along the ground, hasten to the place
with your swiftest wing, for men are surely destroying one another;
you will then find the ground smoking with blood, and covered with
carcasses, of which many are dismembered, and mangled for the
convenience of the vulture."—"But when men have killed their prey,"
said the pupil, "Why do they not eat it?" "When the wolf has killed
a sheep, he suffers not the vulture to touch it till he has satisfied himself.
Is not man another kind of wolf?"—"Man," said the mother, "is the
only beast who kills that which he does not devour, and this quality
makes him so much a benefactor to our species."

In the effort to explain the mystery of human behavior, the mother
quotes a wise old vulture of the Carpathian rocks:

"His opinion was, that man had only the appearance of animal life,
being really vegetables with a power of motion; and that as the boughs
of an oak are dashed together by the storm, that swine may fatten
upon the falling acorns, so men are, by some unaccountable power,
driven one against another, till they lose their motion, that vultures
may be fed. Others think they have observed something of contrivance
and policy among these mischievous beings; and those that hover more
closely round them, pretend, that there is, in every herd, one that gives
directions to the rest, and seems to be more eminently delighted with
a wide carnage. What it is that entitles him to such preëminence we
know not; he is seldom the biggest or the swiftest, but he shows by his
eagerness and diligence that he is, more than any of the others, a friend
to vultures."

The impact of the satire here comes from the ironic point of view. At
first the essay seems not allegorical at all since the animals are not acting
in a way that parallels man's actions. But it turns out that the point of
view itself is an allegory of man's assumption that he is the center of the
universe, with all other beings created for his benefit. This attitude of the
vultures, which is perfectly sustained once Johnson leaves the awkward
introduction of the shepherd for the story itself, contributes an extra
level to the irony of the analysis of the reasons why men kill each other
for the "convenience of the vulture."

In addition to the large body of assorted kinds of fables, there are a
great many more strictly allegorical satires with animal characters. The
very universality and obviousness of the relation of animals to man makes
at once the appeal of this sort of satiric story and its special difficulty.
Both sides of the parallel are so familiar that it is hard to keep them in

proper balance, and every reader feels himself competent from his own observation to judge what the writer is doing with the material. But beyond this recognition of the familiar, there are certain criteria by which to judge success in the form.

One gift essential to the teller of satiric animal tales is the power to keep his reader conscious simultaneously of the human traits satirized and of the animals as animals. The moment he loses hold on resemblance and lets his protagonists become merely animals or merely people, his instrument has slipped in his hands and deflected his material away from satiric allegory into something like *Black Beauty* or *The Three Bears*. But if the writer of animal allegory can successfully sustain and play upon two levels of perception, making us feel that his animals are really animals and yet as human as ourselves, he can control the imaginative response. This doubleness of effect is the central power of great animal stories as different as the *Nun's Priest's Tale* and *The Tar Baby*. We delight in Chaunticleer and Pertelote and Brer Rabbit because they are at once real as people and real as animals. The climax of the Tar Baby story, "Bred en bawn in a brier-patch, Brer Fox—bred en bawn in a brier-patch!" reminds us inescapably that this creature is a rabbit exactly while it reminds us of his resemblance to the human being who by his wit can extricate himself from any difficulty. Uncle Remus concludes, "en wid dat he skip out des ez lively ez a cricket in de embers," and we find his liveliness irresistible because we see a real rabbit skipping off in a mood that we know as human. So with Chaucer's masterpiece: Pertelote's "Pekke hem up right as they growe and ete hem yn" is often cited as one of Chaucer's wittiest reductions to the animal level in all his mock-heroic scheme. Yet this remark, which reminds the reader with humorous felicity that a hen is speaking, conveys also the quintessence of Pertelote's wifely solicitude. It seems that when she is most a chicken, she is most full of the particular sort of femininity that Chaucer is placing beside masculine roosterishness for amused scrutiny.

Indeed, it is belief in these creatures as animals that accentuates and isolates the human trait singled out for laughing observation. The animal make-up from which the human characteristic emerges throws it into high light and sharpens perception, acting as a proper vehicle for the tenor. Thus the true animal allegory fulfills I. A. Richards' requirement: "the vehicle is not . . . a mere embellishment of a tenor which is otherwise unchanged but the vehicle and tenor in co-operation give a meaning of more varied powers than can be ascribed to either." [3]

Since the whole point of animal satire is to show up humanity by revealing human traits in nonhuman characters, it follows that the few human beings who appear must not be characterized at all lest they break into the allegorical scheme. At the end of the Uncle Remus stories we

3. *The Philosophy of Rhetoric* (New York, 1936), p. 100.

know no more about "Miss Meadows en de gals" than does the little boy
when he first asks, "Who was Miss Meadows, Uncle Remus?" and gets
the unenlightening response: "Don't ax me, honey. She wuz in de tale,
Miss Meadows en de gals wuz, en de tale I give you like hi't wer' gun ter
me." The characterization of Mr. Man is if possible even vaguer: "Des
a man, honey. Dat's all." [4] In George Orwell's *Animal Farm,* where the
notion of man as tyrannical master is necessary to the imaginative plan,
the only human character who really figures after the ousting of Mr.
Jones is Whymper, who as his name suggests has no personality at all,
and he is never seen by the nonporcine animals from whose point of view
the story is told. The *Nun's Priest's Tale* may seem an exception to this
rule, for there is a good deal of circumstantial detail in the depicting of
the widow who owns the fowls. But when we come to examine the treatment of her "sooty bower" and her "attempree diete," we find that all the
attention is given to externals. As a person, the widow has no more
identity than do the peasants who own Chaunticleer in Chaucer's sources.
The realistic detail of her few possessions and her meager life is all used
to sharpen the humor of the elaborate mock-heroic treatment of the cock
and his lady. It seems safe to say that there does not exist anywhere a
successful animal allegory which includes a vivid human character.

Another outgrowth of the choice of animal characters to throw human
traits into bold relief is the concentration upon isolated human characteristics. The successful writer of animal allegory rarely gives his characters more than one human trait at a time. This concentrated singleness of attack might almost be laid down as a second law of the genre, as
binding as the first that the animals shall stay both animal and human.
It removes the possibility of very complex characterization. The complexity comes from the double consciousness of animal and human attributes; and the force of the tale is almost in proportion to the singleness
and simplicity on the human level. This is true even of a fairly sustained
piece such as Munro Leaf's *Ferdinand.* The increasingly funny repetition of the comment that Ferdinand just sat down quietly and smelled the
flowers whenever he was expected to fight not only endears the bull to us
in our belligerent world, but leaves the essence of his character indelibly
fixed in our minds. This is all we know of him and all we need to know
except that "He is very happy."

The same practice holds in aggregations of stories centered around one
character such as the medieval beast epic of *Reynard the Fox,* where
Reynard is always cruelly taking advantage of his neighbors, and the
Uncle Remus stories, where Brer Rabbit always mischievously turns the
tables on his stronger enemies. As Uncle Remus puts it, "Eve'y time I
run over in my min' 'bout the pranks er Brer Rabbit . . . hit make me

4. Joel Chandler Harris, *Uncle Remus, His Songs and His Sayings* (New York,
1921), pp. 25, and 143.

laugh mo' en mo'. He mos' allers come out on top, yit dey wuz times w'en he hatter be mighty spry." [5] His invention is boundless, but he is always himself.

> I 'speck dat 'uz de reas'n w'at make ole Brer Rabbit git 'long so well, kaze he aint copy atter none er de yuther creeturs. . . . W'en he make his disappearance 'fo' um, hit 'uz allers in some bran new place. Dey aint know wharbouts fer ter watch out fer 'im. He wuz de funniest creetur er de whole gang. Some folks moughter call him lucky, en yit, w'en he git in bad luck, hit look lak he mos' allers come out on top. Hit look mighty kuse now, but 't wa'n't kuse in dem days, kaze hit 'uz done gun up dat, strike 'im w'en you might en whar you would, Brer Rabbit wuz de soopless creetur gwine. (pp. 21–2)

The essence of his character revealed in story after story Uncle Remus summarizes: "dey w'a'n't no man 'mungs de creeturs w'at kin stan' right flat-footed en wuk he min' quick lak Brer Rabbit." (p. 129) What most stimulates his intelligence is being in a tight place: "Brer Rabbit 'gun ter git skeer'd, en w'en dat creetur git skeer'd, he min' wuk lak one er deze yer flutter-mills." (p. 220)

A corollary of the focus upon single human traits in animal tales is brevity. The swiftness with which the narrative reaches its climax sharpens the concentrated effect of the flashing out of the human motive. Uncle Remus's comment on his hero's character gives the clue to the simple plot of most of his stories, which without ever seeming monotonous repeatedly show Brer Rabbit "monst'us busy . . . sailin' 'roun' fixin' up his tricks" (p. 63) to outdo the other animals who have it in for him: "dem t'er creeturs. Dey wuz allers a-layin' traps fer Brer Rabbit en gittin' cotch in um deyse'f." (p. 119) Though he is usually extricating himself from a difficulty, he sometimes initiates pranks from sheer love of mischief. He is always alert for fun. "Brer Rabbit, he one er deze yer kinder mens w'at sleep wid der eye wide open." (p. 93) The illustrations of his ingenuity as it makes the plots for the tales are endless: he gets Mr. Fox, who has come to fetch him for revenge to serve as his "ridin' hoss" by pretending to be too ill to accompany Brer Fox on foot; he gets Miss Cow stuck fast by the horns in the persimmon tree so that he and all his family can milk her by promising her a feast of persimmons that she is to shake down by butting the tree; he scalds Mr. Wolf, who runs into his chest for protection from the dogs; he gets the bag after Mr. Fox's hunt by playing dead and tempting Brer Fox to add the rabbit to his game; on two occasions he nibbles up the butter and manages to let the 'possum and the weasel have the blame; he saves the meat of his own cow, takes Mr. Man's cow from Brer Fox, and steals Mr. Man's meat and money

---

5. Joel Chandler Harris, *Nights with Uncle Remus* (Boston, 1911), p. 311. All further quotations from *Uncle Remus* are from this edition.

by a series of ruses; he often persuades other animals to take his place in traps by appealing to their greed; he escapes from the hawk by begging to be allowed to grow big enough to make a full meal and from the embrace of the wildcat by offering to tell him how to get turkey meat; he turns the tables on other enemies by appealing to their perversity in many variations on the Tar Baby story. Always Brer Rabbit is equal to the emergency. His own ruses succeed and those to outwit him fail. Only the Terrapin and the Crow ever best him, never any of the stronger animals like the Fox, the Bear, and the Lion. After the account of his exploits, Uncle Remus's judgment seems a model of understatement: "Bless yo' soul, honey, Brer Rabbit mought er bin kinder fibble in de legs, but he w'a'n't no ways cripple und' de hat." (p. 208)

Just as the hero of these stories represents always mischievous fooling, so he confronts only one trait in his antagonist in each story. The singleness of impression, which enforces the sharpness, is never violated. But one source of variety from story to story is the range of human traits singled out in the other creatures for Brer Rabbit's laughter. To be sure, laughter is the quality of his prankish intelligence. "Well . . . you know w'at kinder man Brer Rabbit is. He des went off some 'ers by he own-alone se'f en tuck a big laugh." (p. 214) Uncle Remus's adjective for him is "sassy." But the very story of his Laughing Place is another illustration that the weaknesses of the other creatures give him ample scope to exercise his ingenuity in besting them for his own amusement. Here it is Brer Fox's curiosity that makes him the victim. The stories already mentioned show Brer Rabbit playing upon greed, vanity, eagerness for revenge, or sheer cruelty in his more imposing neighbors. The stories of his frightening the other and bigger animals, even the Lion, by playing upon their natural timorousness are especially striking in view of his own physical helplessness. The Lion lets Brer Rabbit tie him to a tree to save him from being blown away by a nonexistent wind; the animals all run from Brer Rabbit when he appears bedecked in leaves; he scares them from the house they have built by saying that the cannon is his sneeze and the pail of water his spit; he sets a stampede in motion by simply running past and saying he has heard a big noise; and he outdoes himself in frightening the others by the clatter he makes dressed up in the tin plates they are waiting to steal from him:

> Brer Rabbit got right on um 'fo dey kin git away. He holler out, he did:
>
> "Gimme room! Tu'n me loose! I'm ole man Spewter-Splutter wid long claws, en scales on my back! I'm snaggle-toofed en double-jinted! Gimme room!"
>
> Eve'y time he'd fetch a whoop, he'd rattle de cups en slap de platters tergedder—*rickety, rackety, slambang!* En I let you know w'en dem

creeturs got dey lim's tergedder dey split de win', dey did dat. Ole
Brer B'ar, he struck a stump w'at stan' in de way, en I ain't gwine tell
you how he to' it up 'kaze you won't b'leeve me, but de nex' mawnin'
Brer Rabbit en his chilluns went back dar, dey did, en dey got nuff
splinters fer ter make um kin'lin' wood all de winter. (p. 123)

The human bully is probably the character most roundly mocked by Brer
Rabbit.

In Caxton's version of the medieval stories of Reynard, on the other
hand, the hero is the bully. Surely from the folklorist's viewpoint one of
the most interesting aspects of animal stories is the relationships among
the various groups. The story of Brer Rabbit's rising from the well by
getting the fox to leap into the other well bucket, for instance, is identical
with the story that Erswynd, wife of Isegrim the Wulf, tells of her being
tricked into the well bucket by Reynard. A plot that is repeated with
different characters in both sets of stories is that of the creature delivered
and turning on his deliverer, only to be re-imprisoned by the judgment
of a third party. Rukenaw tells in Caxton the story of the man's freeing
the serpent, who then turns on the man, with Reynard as the judge who
refuses advice until he sees the contestants in their original positions. In
the Uncle Remus version, the creature under the rock is the wolf, who is
freed by Brer Rabbit, and the judge is Brer Tarrypin (always Brer
Rabbit's ally except when he outruns his speedier friend in the Uncle
Remus variant of the story of the Tortoise and the Hare) who says: "I
hates might'ly fer ter put you all gents ter so much trouble; yit, dey aint
no two ways, I'll hatter see des how Brer Wolf was kotch, en des how de
rock wuz layin' 'pun top un 'im." (p. 278) Then of course the wolf is left
pinned under the rock just as is the snake in the other story.

The intricate ramifications of interrelations of sources for both sets of
stories lie beyond the scope of this study, which is concerned with the
artistry of the telling. But the subject of the representation of the heroes
is an aesthetic problem which is curiously linked with the larger anthro-
pological relation. It is hard to resist the impression that somewhere in
the course of the development of the two groups of tales, one hero was set
up in deliberate response to the other. Both are extremely clever; and both
triumph over the other animals by deceits. But the feeling created by the
two is totally different. When Uncle Remus says, "dat seetful Brer
Rabbit done fool ole Brer Fox" (p. 89), we laugh with the rabbit. When
Erswynd says, "Ache felle reynart / noman can kepe hym self fro the[e]
/ thou canst so wel vttre thy wordes and thy falsenes and reson sette
forth," [6] our sympathy is all with the duped she-wolf. Instead of rejoicing
at Reynard's triumphs, the reader shudders at the cruelty of his tricks,

6. Quotations are from *The History of Reynard the Fox, translated and printed by
William Caxton,* ed. Edward Arber (London, 1880), pp. 96 and 71.

which grow in evil from his making Bruin lose "his scalp, ears, and fore-paws," in his bloody escape "nearly dead" from the cloven tree, through his preparing for his false pilgrimage by securing a square foot of Bruin's hide for his scrip and two shoes from each by ripping off the pawskins of Isegrim and Erswynd, through his cold-blooded devouring of Cuwart, the Hare, to the horrors of the final fight in which he slips his shaved and oiled body always out of Isegrim's grasp while he blinds the wolf by slap-ping his face with the tail befouled according to Rukenaw's suggestion, kicking sand into Isegrim's eyes, and treating him with every sort of indignity until he wins with his ugly stratagem leaving Isegrim mutilated and half dead. Parallel to the mounting cruelty of his deeds is the increas-ing baseness of his false speeches. His deceits instead of tickling the fancy like those of Brer Rabbit make their treachery abhorrent. There is serious hatred of Reynard and serious reason for it:

> Alle the beestis both poure and riche were alle stylle when the foxe spak so stoutly / the cony laprel and the roek were so sore aferde that they durste not speke but pyked and stryked them out of the court bothe two. and whan they were a room fer in the playne they saide. god graunte that this felle murderare may fare euyl. he can bywrappe and couere his falshede. that his wordes seme as trewe as the gospel herof knoweth noman than we. how shold we brynge wytnesse. it is better that we wyke and departe. than we sholde holde a felde and fyghte with hym. he is so shrewde. ye[a] thaugh ther of vs were fyue we coude not defende vs. but he shold sle vs alle.

While the narrative management in *Reynard the Fox*, as in other groups of animal stories is episodic, Caxton's version of the epic has de-cided organization toward a climax. The increasing tension is craftily arranged. Reynard's first false defense is filled with consummate treach-ery; but his villainy is greater in his second hoodwinking of the king. When honors are finally heaped upon him after his foul play to Isegrim, perfidy is left triumphant. If we turn from such a spectacle of evil to the merry pranks of Brer Rabbit, we are bound to feel some slight restoring of poetic justice in the fact that Brer Fox is always defeated in his efforts to outwit Brer Rabbit. Nothing can bring to life the hens and pigeons and other helpless creatures, even Cuwart the Hare himself, whom Reynard has foully murdered; but it is hard to resist the feeling that the sly Brer Fox is suffering some retribution for the sins of Reynard.

This strong difference in response to the two protagonists suggests a third criterion by which to judge the satirist using animal tales for his allegory. The kinds of smartness displayed by Reynard and Brer Rabbit are, of course, different; but much of the difference in the feeling about them is determined by the attitude toward them displayed in the stories. The establishing of a clear point of view toward the animal characters seems as important a requisite for the successful animal tale as does the focusing on a single dominant trait in the animal. The rejoicing of Uncle Remus and his various hearers iñ the exploits of Brer Rabbit is an incalculable aid to Harris in communicating the same attitude to the reader; but as he repeatedly says in the introductions to his various volumes, he did not create Uncle Remus's point of view. Brer Rabbit is the hero, in the full admiring sense of the word, of the stories as Harris heard them told by Negro after Negro. To be sure, he is a hero that can be laughed at; but the gay satire is directed at the human foibles of the other animals which lead them into Brer Rabbit's traps. In the stories of Reynard, on the other hand, while there is some mockery of the animals who are Reynard's dupes, the appalling comment on human character comes in Reynard himself. Modern experience of the rise of tyrants through cruelty and lies must intensify response to the revelation of iniquity in Reynard; but there can be no doubt that Caxton intends Reynard to be regarded as a villain. We see that Isegrim is as simple-minded as Brer Wolf; but instead of feeling that his stupidity is mocked, we resent the violence done him. We are conscious of the greed of Bruin and Tybert which helps make them prey to Reynard's wiles; Bellin's desire for importance is directly responsible for his being killed as Cuwart's murderer; and Nobel seems a very unsuspecting monarch indeed to be taken in by Reynard's flattery. But many of the fox's victims have no other weakness than physical helplessness. The revealing light of the allegorical satire is turned most searchingly upon the villainous hero himself; and when he is allowed to go off triumphant in the end, the feeling is that the wicked ways of the world have been convincingly displayed.

There is obviously a good deal of social satire, especially of abuses in the church, in *Reynard the Fox*. This would be in a measure true of any group of stories presenting a number of animals together. The mere assembling of individuals suggests some comment on social structure. Even the fables of La Fontaine display the classes of society, as does the assembly of birds alone in *The Parlement of Foules*. But in some animal stories, the central purpose is clearly comment on society rather than on individual human traits. In such stories the same artistic criteria hold. The sustaining of the animal disguise is still the first requisite; the absence of strong human characters and the presence of sharply individualized animal characters with a single dominant human trait seem as important for the social satire couched in animal terms as for the story whose object is simply laughter at a human foible; a clear viewpoint again must control the response. The failure to meet these tests of the successful writer of animal allegory explains the ineptitudes of so great an allegorist as Spenser when he tries to tell an animal story.

Mother Hubberds Tale, for all its vivid picture of abuses in church and court, is not a successful animal satire. The Fox and the Ape are specious rogues indeed, but we never believe in them as animals except possibly for the moment of their stealing the Lion's skin. Many similarities have been shown between Spenser's material and that of the medieval stories of Reynard, including the basic one of alliance in trickery of these two animals.[7] But Spenser never succeeds in giving them the life of their prototypes. Part of his difficulty in giving his characters reality as animals may come from his being unable to transmute the images of real men. It seems clear that the animals stand for actual individuals at Elizabeth's court, though scholars dispute about the identification of the Ape. The result of their not becoming convincing animal characters is that the poem affords none of the pleasure of using the imagination at two levels, which is the chief reason for being of allegory. When Spenser's protagonists trick the husbandman into hiring them as shepherd and dog, they are simply thieves who enjoy stealing and slaying the sheep. They do eat the flock; but there is no distinction between the eating done by Ape and Fox, for they are both all the while simply deceitful men. In the final episode when they come to rule, with the Ape in the stolen skin of the Lion, we forget altogether that it is a lion's throne they have usurped and are given almost a lecture on the abuses of false human courtiers and the pitiful plight of suitors at court, with the lesson pointed by the contrasting picture of the man who truly loves honor. Spenser is writing here with too much passion of personal disillusion to achieve artistic detachment and the indirection of allegory. Animals are forgotten in lines like these:

> Most miserable man, whom wicked fate
> Hath brought to Court, to sue for had ywist,
> That few haue found, and manie one hath mist;
> Full little knowest thou that hast not tride,
> What hell it is, in suing long to bide:
> To loose good dayes, that might be better spent;
> To wast long nights in pensiue discontent;
> To speed to day, to be put back to morrow;
> To feed on hope, to pine with feare and sorrow;
> To haue thy Princes grace, yet want her Peeres;
> To haue thy asking, yet waite manie yeeres;
> To fret thy soule with crosses and with cares;
> To eate thy heart through comfortlesse dispaires;
> To fawne, to crowche, to waite, to ride, to ronne,
> To spend, to giue, to want, to be vndonne.
> Vnhappie wight, borne to desastrous end,
> That doth his life in so long tendance spend.
> (ll. 892–908, Variorum ed.)

7. Cf. Edwin Greenlaw, "The Sources of Spenser's 'Mother Hubberd's Tale,'" *Modern Philology, 2* (1905), 411–32.

It is, in fact, startling to return to the story of the sleeping Lion by the awkward device of having Jove send Mercury to awaken him and spur him back to his kingdom to drive out the usurpers. The encounter with the priest whom the Fox and the Ape meet between their tricks as shepherds and as courtiers is a sharply ironic indictment of the worldly practices of churchmen. But the account of the proper way to make a priest's life a soft one is put into the mouth of a real priest, who is all too convincingly human. Consequently, we almost nowhere feel that we are in an animal world; and when Sir Mule or the sheep whose lamb the wolf has killed does appear as an actual animal, we are startled and jarred. *Mother Hubberds Tale* is almost as far from being true animal allegory as is *The Hind and the Panther*. The force of Spenser's satiric feeling and the variety of his poetic power carry us along; but the poem does not succeed as a work of art.

George Orwell, a writer of much less stature than Spenser, has written in *Animal Farm* a more effective social satire than *Mother Hubberds Tale*. His animals are absolutely real as animals from the first meeting in the big barn to hear Old Major's dream of a world in which the animals are equal and free of their human masters to their frightened approach to the farmhouse window at the end of the book when only those animals who are tall enough can peep in. The horses are always horses who pull loads; the cows are cows who must be milked, however awkwardly, by the pigs, "their trotters being well adapted to this task"; [8] the hens are hens who lay eggs and want to keep them; even the bureaucratic pigs remain pigs, hard as they try to be human—which gives its overwhelming force to the denouément of the story when the terrified subject animals creep back to the window of the farmhouse and look "from pig to man, and from man to pig, and from pig to man again; but already it [is] impossible to say which [is] which." (p. 118)

The point of view is always that of the animals who are being duped. Their plight is deepened for the reader by his being allowed to discover the successive machinations of the pigs only as they are borne in upon the stupider animals. Orwell never forgets and lets us inside the consciousness of Napoleon and Squealer. We simply see the one strutting and lording it over his victims and hear the other giving specious explanations of why the pigs must live in luxury. We see and hear what the subject animals see and hear.

While they are consistently animals, each reveals a predominant human trait. Clover is a "stout motherly mare" from the time when at the opening meeting she makes a protecting wall around the motherless ducklings with her great foreleg, through the time after the purge when

8. George Orwell, *Animal Farm* (New York, 1946), p. 22. All quotations are from this edition.

the desolate survivors huddle around her, and through her efforts to keep Boxer from overworking and then to rescue him from the knacker, until she leads her fearful fellow creatures up to the farmhouse at the end, to witness the full extent of their betrayal.

Boxer "was not of first-rate intelligence, but he was universally respected for his steadiness of character and tremendous powers of work." (p. 4) His inability to learn the alphabet is linked with his unswerving devotion to his two mottoes: "I will work harder" and "Comrade Napoleon is always right," for there is something stupid in his letting his great strength be used up to serve the interests of the oppressors in the totalitarian state. Yet his loyalty is intensely moving, especially as his strength fails and he still works harder than ever: "Sometimes on the slope leading to the top of the quarry, when he braced his muscles against the weight of some vast boulder, it seemed that nothing kept him on his feet except the will to continue. At such times his lips were seen to form the words, 'I will work harder'; he had no voice left." (p. 98) And when in the knacker's van the drumming of his hoofs grows fainter and dies away, we feel all the force of human goodness traduced so that after the faithful horse has been made into glue and dog meat, there is all the greater sense of outrage at Squealer's fraudulent speech to the Comrades distorting all the circumstances of Boxer's life and death (for which he makes up a sentimental deathbed scene in a beautifully tended hospital instead of the actual slaughter house one) to make the other animals more servile slaves than ever.

The delineation of a single human trait is just as vivid in the other animals: the boar Snowball, the impetuous, inventive leader who is ousted; the other boar Napoleon the dictator, who starts out by taking the milk and apples for the pigs and goes on to the creating of a slave state; Squealer, the pig propagandist, who shifts the commandments to suit the leaders' actions and explains all their oppressions as to the advantage of the comrades; the donkey Benjamin, who is a cynic; Mollie, the pretty white mare who loves ribbons more than principle; and all the others. Even the animals who are not named and appear in groups show up human crowds in single moods. The silly sheep always bleat at the pigs' command, whether their tune is "Four legs good, two legs bad" or "Four legs good, two legs better." The terrible dogs trained as Napoleon's bodyguard are always the ferocious, bloodthirsty instruments of terror. They are the police of the police state.

Since Orwell has succeeded in his underlining of separate human characteristics in his individual animals, his comment on society is convincing. It is because the imaginative scheme of the animal allegory is sustained that the revelation of the ease with which well-meaning citizens can be duped into serving the masters of a totalitarian state achieves its power. Orwell's keeping the point of view consistently that of the help-less animals and letting us make only the discoveries that they make forces us to interpret for ourselves not just the misfortunes of the renamed Manor Farm, but also those of our own world. We are compelled to par-ticipate imaginatively. *Animal Farm* is successful social satire because it is successful allegory.

5

Satiric Journeys I: Gulliver's Travels

*"Some cross the sea to see strange lands unknown
And here like strangers do not know their own."*
JOHN TAYLOR

SO FAR the allegorical schemes considered have stayed within the
known world, perhaps shedding the light that never was on land
or sea upon the familiar, but nevertheless remaining on this earth.
The stories which parallel human action, the adventures of mock heroes,
the behavior of animals with the traits of men, all take place in recogniz-
able scenes. The allegorical satirist more often, however, resorts to the
creation of a wholly new frame of reference. He delights in making up a
fantastic world to reveal the truth as he sees it about the known world.
This kind of intensification is so common that it can be spoken of as the
distinctive method of satire "with its mixing up of *worlds,* its concealment
of one world behind another." [1] The varieties of ways in which the
imagination of the satirist plays with fantasy are almost endless, so that
it is impossible to group and categorize satires projected in terms of
strange worlds. One basic division, nevertheless, may be useful for purposes of discussion. Fundamentally, the satirist who wishes to depart
from this world in order to reveal it must go away either in time or in
space. Thus the creators of fantastic voyages make a geographical departure; the prophets of future worlds make a temporal one. The satiric
journey which stands so pre-eminent as to fix the conception of the type
is *Gulliver's Travels.*

Like many another short title, *Gulliver* is misleading. Swift's own
title, *Travels into several Remote Nations of the World,* gives a truer
notion of the imaginative intent of the work. The appearance of Lemuel
Gulliver, "First a Surgeon, and then a Captain of several Ships," on the
original title page only as author defines his artistic function. His character is important in determining the point of view; but it is by means of
his travels that his creator projects both the allegory and the satire: the
satire through the allegory. In selecting the journey as an artistic form,
Swift adopts a medium which is thoroughly familiar in both satiric and

1. P. N. Furbank, *Samuel Butler* (Cambridge, 1948), p. 27.

religious allegory. He has many predecessors in the use of the imaginary journey for comment on conditions in this world; and the usefulness of such an allegorical scheme for his own purpose is manifest. His youthful experiment with political allegory in *Contests and Dissensions in Athens and Rome* had taught him the value of a more flexible form. He was to adhere all his life to the views expressed in that early work; but for the projection of his maturest satire, the parallels fixed by ancient history would have been too rigid. The voyage form gave him complete freedom to express his own views and yet enabled him to appeal to all the ready-made response to the very word *travel*.

He himself had steadily felt the fascination of books of actual travel,[2] and could therefore the better take satiric advantage of their enormous popularity. Swift's participation in the feeling which made Dampier in particular so seize upon the contemporary imagination is demonstrated by the way he plays upon and uses it for his own purposes. He capitalizes to the full on the desire for vicarious experience, the already existing will to believe. With characteristic doubleness of intention, he can mock the real mariner's concern with trifles and his reader's appetite for them, even while feeding and counting upon that appetite. The most familiar example of this sort of dry mock is his taking the description of the storm from Sturmy's *Mariner's Magazine* for the opening of Book II. The parody is the more delightful because it is still half actually in the spirit of the original: the shifted attitude is perceived only in relation to the rest of the tale. Swift is in part sincerely delighted with all the wealth of extravagant literalness and expects his reader to be. And his pleasure in realistic detail is partly what enables him to achieve the circumstantiality that is so often pointed out as giving credibility to his imaginary lands.

There is something of the same self-mockery in the parody of the scrupulous accuracy of the voyagers in setting down their observations according to the directions of the Royal Society:

> Let them therefore always have a Table-Book at hand to set down every thing worth remembring, and then at night more methodically transcribe the Notes they have taken in the day. The principal Heads by which to regulate their Observations are these, the Climate, Government, Power, Places of Strength, Cities of note, Religion, Language, Coins, Trade, Manufactures, Wealth, Bishopricks, Universities, Antiquities, Libraries, Collections of Rarities, Arts and Artists, Publick Structures, Roads, Bridges, Woods, Mountains, Customs, Habits, Laws, Privileges, strange Adventures, surprising Accidents,

2. The evidence of his interest is compactly summarized by Harold Williams in his introduction to *Gulliver's Travels, The Prose Works of Jonathan Swift*, ed. Herbert Davis (Oxford, 1941), *11*, xiv–xvi. All references to *Gulliver's Travels* are to this edition.

Rarities both natural and artificial, the Soil, Plants, Animals, and whatsoever may be curious, diverting, or profitable . . . Every Traveller ought to carry about him several sorts of Measures, to take the Dimensions of such things as require it; a Watch by which, and the Pace he travels, he may give some guess at the distances of Places . . . a Prospective-glass, or rather a great one and a less, to take views of Objects at greater and less distances; a small Sea-Compass or Needle, to observe the situation of Places, and a parcel of the best Maps to make curious Remarks of their exactness, and note down where they are faulty. In fine, a Traveller must endeavour to see the Courts of Princes, to keep the best Company, and to converse with the most celebrated Men in all Arts and Sciences.[3]

Swift makes Gulliver follow these directions to the letter. It is the scrupulousness with which he endeavors to "keep the best Company" that leads him finally to disaster. The heads of his observations correspond so closely to those in the directions that he seems to be recounting his travels by their formula. He records his use of his small pocket perspective glass, part of the prescribed equipment, to spy out the fleet of Blefuscu, to reach the flying island, and to leave the land of the Houyhnhnms. He is extremely careful about estimating distances and concerned for the improvement of maps. He points out the error of geographers in "supposing nothing but Sea between *Japan* and *California*" (p. 95) and is annoyed that his corrections about New-Holland are not put to use: "This confirmed me in the Opinion I have long entertained, that the *Maps* and *Charts* place this Country at least three Degrees more to the *East* than it really is; which Thought I communicated many Years ago to my worthy Friend Mr. *Herman Moll,* and gave him my Reasons for it, although he hath rather chosen to follow other Authors." (p. 268) Swift's voyager is imbued with the spirit inculcated by the Royal Society and bent on making his observations useful as well as accurate.

Yet Swift's laughter at the minuteness of Gulliver's concern and the kind of detail he is accurate about is partly at his own expense. The closeness of Gulliver's scrutiny of externals might be taken as an ironic symbol of Swift's examination of human motive. Swift is voyaging in stranger seas than Gulliver is. But he is also enjoying the carefully worked out record of the supposed travels. He can parody the literalness of manner of the actual travel books while using the apparent simplicity with the most artful design.

Gulliver's friend Herman Moll may have furnished Swift with some of the particulars which Gulliver records. In Moll's Atlas of 1709 there is the large promise of

3. John Churchill, *A Collection of Voyages and Travels* (London, 1704), I, lxxv–lxxvi. Quoted by R. W. Frantz, *The English Traveller and the Movement of Ideas 1660–1732, University Studies* (University of Nebraska, 1934), pp. 23–4.

The World described; or, a New and Correct Sett of Maps: shewing,
The Kingdoms and States in all the known Parts of the Earth, with
the principal Cities, and most considerable Towns in the World.
Wherein the Errors of the antient *Geographers* are corrected according to the latest Observations of Travellers, as Communicated to the
Royal Society of *London,* and the *Royal Academy* of *Paris.* Each Map
is neatly engraved on Copper by Herman Moll, *Geographer,* and
printed on two sheets of Elephant-Paper, so that the Scale is large
enough to shew the chief Cities and Towns, as well as Provinces, without appearing in the least confus'd. And to render these Maps the more
acceptable, there is engraved on several of them what is most remarkable in those Countries.

The pictures of what is most remarkable abound in strange suggestions.
The set accompanying the map of Denmark and Sweden is headed: "The
Laplanders being the most Remarkable People in Europe; it will not be
amiss to give a Scheach of their manner of Living." The picture labeled
in the key, "Their way of Burying," shows four naked figures standing
bolt upright in a picketed enclosure and another equally erect in a tall
box. Clearly all five are waiting to rise. This could conceivably be what
Swift sees upside down when he says of the Lilliputians: "They bury
their Dead with their Heads directly downwards; because they hold an
Opinion, that in eleven Thousand Moons they are all to rise again; in
which Period, the Earth (which they conceive to be flat) will turn upside
down, and by this Means they shall, at their Resurrection, be found ready
standing on their Feet." (pp. 41–2) The pictures include many of
strange animals; the one of "The Dominions of the King of Great
Britain on ye Continent of North America" shows beavers making a
dam. They are displayed in various stages of building with logs that recall the Houyhnhnm carpentry. Many of the maps have sketches of cities
which make Swift's comment on Mildendo leap to mind: "I viewed the
Town on my left Hand, which looked like the painted Scene of a city in a
Theatre." (p. 13) The lamps in the picture of the Holy Sepulchre give
immediately the effect of those in the Astronomer's Cave of Laputa. It
would be surprising if the range of Moll's pictures of "what is most remarkable" had not made a strong impression upon an imagination like
Swift's which habitually seized on material in out of the way places and
used it in fresh combinations. Such use of actual material of travel for
parody or for realistic detail is one of the marks of originality in *Gulliver's Travels.*

Swift differs markedly from other writers of imaginary voyages not
only in making adroit use of real travels, but also in clarity of allegorical
intent. One reads Lucian's *True History* in a spirit of sheer merriment.
The parodist gives warning: "But my lying is far more honest than

theirs, for though I tell truth in nothing else, I shall at least be truthful in saying that I am a liar. I think I can escape the censure of the world by my own admission that I am not telling a word of truth." [4] Consequently, while we perceive his mockery of the historians, we read on, expecting the kind of irresponsible fun he gives: fish that have the effect of wine, grapevines that have the bodies of women, grassplume riders and flea archers, ant dragoons and vulture dragoons, and even life within the whale. We think very little of the stories as mockery of historians' fanciful tales because we are too preoccupied with them as fanciful tales themselves. There is interest in speculating about how some of Lucian's extravagant details wrought upon the imagination of the creator of *Gulliver's Travels.* Do the ears of plane leaves and the removable eyes, for instance, suggest the senses that are usable only with the help of flappers in Laputa? [5] But the charm of Lucian is the feeling of pure caprice, the sharing of his own joy in prodigal invention, with occasional comment on mankind tossed in apparently just for an extra fillip of interest. The parallels with Swift throw into startling relief Swift's controlled precision of meaning. This is just as true of the two books which D'Ablancourt added to his French translation of Lucian. Lively as D'Ablancourt's imagination is, he appears still freer than Lucian of consistent allegorical or satiric intent. Swift's pleasure in these imaginary voyages must have been very much like our own, a pleasure in fancy itself rather than in its use for a purpose. The parallels from Cyrano de Bergerac are even more impressive. But Cyrano, like Lucian, is capricious in his management of implication in his voyages, though he is sharper than Lucian in his condemnation of man, and it is man as man that is condemned rather than as historian or literary commentator. Again there are details which tease the student of Swift with questions as to how much lurked in Swift's mind to appear transformed in *Gulliver.* The insistence on simplicity of language and its relation to truth in Books II and IV, for instance, gives added interest to Cyrano's "qui rencontre cette verité de lettres, de mots, & de suite, ne peut jamais en s'exprimant tomber au dessous de sa conception, il parle toûjours égal à sa pensée; & c'est pour n'avoir pas la connoissance de ce parfait idiôme, que vous demeurez court, ne conoissant pas l'ordre ny les paroles qui puissant expliquer ce que vous imaginez." [6] But simplicity with its basis in exactness is one of the principles emphasized in the "Proposal for Correcting, Improving, and Ascertaining the English Tongue," written long before Swift evolved the language of Brobdingnag with its guttural appropriateness to the giants, or of Houyhnhnm land with its many *h*'s and *y*'s to suggest

4. *A True Story,* tr. A. M. Harmon (Loeb Classics), *1,* 253.

5. More striking recollections of Lucian in *Gulliver* are cited by W. A. Eddy, *Gulliver's Travels, A Critical Study* (Princeton, 1923), pp. 53-5.

6. *Les Oeuvres de Monsieur Cyrano de Bergerac,* seconde partie (Paris, 1676), pp. 215-16.

the whinny of a horse. It is indeed but another statement of Swift's "proper words in proper places." Clearly we do not have to do with a source in Cyrano. However amusing it is to hunt for similarities of detail, there was little Swift could have learned from his so-called sources about the solving of the specific problems of allegorical satire in the imaginary journey.

The first of these is perhaps the establishment of the underlying intent. How soon and how directly can the writer of such a voyage let the reader know what he is up to? By what methods is he to reveal so that the reader will have the pleasure of seeming to find out for himself what is hidden? Since the great pleasure of both allegory and satire, and hence peculiarly of allegorical satire, is being in the secret, laughing with a "few friends in a corner," the mystery must be present and it must also be clear to the astute. An unanswered riddle misses its purpose; but a riddle which is too easy is just as much a failure among the elect as is one that is too hard among the vulgar. What is the right degree of difficulty? The moment of time between the perception of the outward seeming and the perception of the underlying intent, which makes the great charm of all speaking by indirection and which through its sharpening of the barb becomes the special means of economy in satiric allegory, if it is prolonged, makes for diffusion instead of intensification and hence for artistic waste rather than economy. The pitfall is especially treacherous in the initial stage of the voyage, for if the writer waits too long to disclose that he has something in view beyond his apparent purpose, the story itself may so beguile the reader as to keep him from being aware of the first hints of allegory and satire. But to begin with, the participation of the reader must be engaged.

The initial winning of confidence Swift triumphantly achieves. Part of what enables him to do this is his adopting the plainness of style urged upon actual travelers by the Royal Society, the serious dispatch with which Gulliver recites facts that could be true in the life of any adventurous plain man, a man of something of Defoe's class and temperament, and then begins to inject impossible elements. Another part is due to Swift's power to communicate physical sensation. His use of detail is far more than the heaping up of circumstantial evidence for the sake of verisimilitude, which might be the mark of Gulliver's style as mariner. Swift has a purpose beyond this: through what Gulliver straightforwardly sets down for the sake of the record, his creator recaptures the physical experience. The hyperacuteness of Swift's bodily senses has often been pointed out; the intensity of his imagination—visual and auditory and olfactory and motor—is just as acute. His habit of "perceiving absent things as if they were present" suffuses such a work, for instance, as the *Journal to Stella:* "I was speaking monkey things in air, just as if MD had been by," "when I am writing in our language I make up my mouth just as if I was speaking it." "No, faith, you are just here upon this little paper, and therefore I see and talk with you every evening constantly." [7] Consequently, in such a work as *Gulliver,* he makes the reader see and feel because he has first seen and felt himself. Gulliver says:

> I attempted to rise, but was not able to stir: For as I happened to lie on my Back, I found my Arms and Legs were strongly fastened on each Side to the Ground; and my Hair, which was long and thick, tied down in the same Manner. I likewise felt several slender Ligatures across my Body, from my Armpits to my Thighs. I could only look upwards; the Sun began to grow hot, and the Light offended mine Eyes. I heard a confused Noise about me, but in the Posture I lay, could see nothing except the Sky. In a little time I felt something alive moving on my left Leg, which advancing gently forward over my Breast, came almost up to my Chin; when bending mine Eyes downwards as much as I could, I perceived it to be a human Creature not six Inches high, with a Bow and Arrow in his Hands, and a Quiver at his Back. (pp. 5–6)

Swift makes the reader feel the very straining of Gulliver's muscles as he tries to see what is on his chest.

Compelling the reader to such participation is an accomplishment of no mean order; but Swift has a harder kind of suspension of disbelief to achieve. He must win acceptance of the sensuously perceived narrative as something more than itself, and he must do it early if he is not to be misleading about his purpose and so cause resistance when he does call attention to the meaning. This more difficult and peculiarly allegorical task he likewise accomplishes. The idea that the book is more than a story is so familiar that it is almost impossible to judge on its merits the revelation of purpose within the narrative. But unmistakable hints come very early. From the first perception of the first Lilliputian, the reader is invited to consider humankind: "I perceived it to be a human Creature not six Inches high." Swift makes here a plain declaration that his subject is man and the littleness of man. And as the opening scene unfolds, there are constant reminders that it is human actions and human attitudes that make it up: "they shot another Flight into the Air, as we do Bombs in *Europe*"; "He acted every part of an Orator; and I could observe many Periods of Threatnings, and others of Promises, Pity, and Kindness." "I could not sufficiently wonder at the Intrepidity of these diminutive Mortals." The uncanny recognition of these as indeed human creatures not six inches high is as much a part of the spell cast by the opening chapters as is the feeling that they actually exist. Thus even in the first chap-

7. *Journal to Stella,* ed. Harold Williams (Oxford, 1948), *1,* 154–5, 210, and 232.

ter the curiosity of the rabble and the mischievous tickling of Gulliver's
nose with the pikestaff clearly portray human traits, though they emerge
sharpened by the allegorical perspective of Lilliputian size.

Before long Swift creates awareness that, in conjunction with the
steady revelation of human characteristics, he is intermittently satirizing
particular actions of particular men. The obvious reference of the examination of Gulliver's pockets to political investigations immediately sets
the mind to work upon specific applications. Consequently, by the time
the third chapter launches into accounts of the acrobatic feats to attain
office, we are prepared to identify Flimnap and the king's cushion and
the other echoes of English politics which Swift begins to inject. This
gradual initiating of the reader into successive layers of meaning is part
of Swift's adroitness in the management of allegory. We do not know
at once that Lilliput is England, but we do know almost at once that the
Lilliputians are human beings revealing human follies with all the clarity
that the shifted scale of Lilliputian size makes possible. Later, when we
have made this adjustment, we begin to get particular references that are
unmistakable. The reader is flattered by being let into one secret after
another, seeing first through the nature of the Lilliputians into the nature
of man and then through the happenings at their court into events in
England; and two compliments to the understanding are more beguiling
than one.

Another problem with which Swift must deal is the question of how
much weight of meaning the story can bear, the constant problem of the
allegorist, which is especially pressing if the allegory is satiric. Must the
writer adhere steadily to his allegorical scheme? Furthermore, it is part
of the embarrassing richness of allegory as a medium that it can give
concrete representation at once to other concretes and to the larger truth
involved. If the allegory is to carry two levels of satiric ideas, should
they be perceived simultaneously through a given episode? Should both
be present in every episode which is made to bear either? *Gulliver's
Travels* provides interesting answers to these questions.

As to the first, Swift obviously felt no compulsion to adhere steadily
to the allegorical scheme. He makes two quite different kinds of departures from it, with complete success in one kind and mixed success in the
other. Much of *Gulliver* is not allegorical and not satiric, but simply part
of the management of the impression of a realistic narrative. Since the
underlying allegoric and satiric intent has been so early and so clearly
established, we are not bothered by particulars for which no meaning
beyond the surface one appears. Indeed the blend of straight story with
allegory saves the formula from rigidity and helps the narrative to carry
the meaning by making it convincing in itself. No one would willingly
part with unallegorical details such as the accounts of Gulliver's contrivance of his stools for getting into the courts of the Lilliputian emperor's

palace or of his oaten cakes and rush mats in the land of the Houyhnhnms.

But Swift makes another sort of break in his allegorical scheme by thrusting in straight analysis of his ideas. Since this is a direct appeal to the intellect and moral judgment, it is a much more dangerous sort of intrusion than are the narrative details which stay within the province of the imagination. In this bolder interruption of his allegory, Swift is only partially successful. The first part of the sixth chapter of the Voyage to Lilliput halts the allegory in a way that suggests interpolation of an essay which Swift (rather than Gulliver) could not bear to leave out. Case does not explain away its awkwardness by saying: "At this point Swift, to heighten suspense, interpolates a chapter on general conditions of life in Lilliput, which, while it contains a number of isolated satiric references, does not advance the main plot." [8] It is not actually a chapter on general conditions, for if these conditions prevailed, the people would be far better than Swift has depicted them as being. This is especially true in the realm of education. He is far from having shown the Lilliputians as the products of the system he describes. The account reads like "An Essay on Modern Education" in reverse and is clearly Swift's idea of what ought to be done, not of what is done in Lilliput or anywhere else. Swift himself in his apology for the chapter does not claim that it describes general conditions but rather the original purity from which the institutions have fallen away. It can hardly be brought into the unity of Book I, though it may sharpen the excitement of the surrounding narrative by its lack of action. Its justification is rather its relation to the body of positive idea that is the basis of the whole satire; but this is scarcely an artistic justification. Once the discourse on education is over, Swift retires, and we hear again the voice of Gulliver: "AND here it may perhaps divert the curious Reader, to give some Account of my Domestick, and my Manner of living in this Country during a Residence of nine Months and thirteen Days." (p. 47)

There are several places where instead of a direct account of ideal conditions, Swift makes a direct account of conditions that exist or have existed in the real world. The least successful part of the third voyage is the visit to Glubdubdrib, where Gulliver is simply learning—or mislearning—the lessons of history with the device of the magicians almost forgotten. It is Swift who is summoning these ghosts without any real attempt to do it through allegorical indirection. The comparative dulness of the direct statement of the morals to be drawn from the figures of antiquity is emphasized by the placing of the visit to Glubdubdrib immediately after the chapters on the Grand Academy of Lagado, where Swift is content to laugh at misuses of the mind in general and the Royal Society in particular without once breaking into the allegory. He does not need to interpret the images of stupidity in which he has set forth the

8. A. E. Case, *Four Essays on Gulliver's Travels* (Princeton, 1945), p. 76.

projectors. The engine for grinding words into books is an allegory of
which the tenor is familiar in its sinister emphasis and yet is made fresh
and more distressing by the vehicle Swift gives it. The mechanicalness of
the actions of the professor and his pupils and Gulliver's solemn recording
give an appropriate flatness to the presentation of the renunciation of the
power of the writer to create. As Gulliver records the experiments to make
cloth of cobwebs and produce a breed of naked sheep, Swift uses exactly
the tone of the Transactions of the Royal Society which he is parodying.
Because the allegory is sustained in the treatment of the Academy, it is
one of the most successful parts of the uneven third voyage, just as the
episode of the magicians is one of its weakest parts for the contrary reason.

The analyses of conditions in England which are made by the King of
Brobdingnag and Gulliver's master in the land of the Houyhnhnms after
Gulliver's accounts of his native land bear a skillfully mixed relation to
the allegory. The fiction of a conversation is carefully preserved in each
case; and the obliquity of the treatment of England is much greater in
the fourth book, where the much greater length of the comment makes it
more necessary. In the conversation with the King of Brobdingnag, the
only indirection comes from Gulliver's unwitting betrayal of the vices of
his countrymen and the penetrating questions of the king which lead up
to his contemptuous denunciation of "the most pernicious Race of little
odious Vermin." The account itself is moderate enough, and in fact
Gulliver considers it a panegyric, explaining that he has given as favor-
able an account as possible even while he repudiates the king's judgment:
"it would be hard indeed, if so remote a Prince's Notions of Virtue and
Vice were to be offered as a Standard for all Mankind." (p. 117) The
king's attitude is indeed Olympian and prepares for the cool judgment
of reason itself from Gulliver's horse master.

The conversation in Book IV is nearly five times as long, and contains
great variety of relation to the allegorical scheme. It is fundamentally
different from the conversation in Book II in not starting from a fair
account of England. Gulliver is now seeing with the eyes of the emotion-
less horses and hence in the interest of truth gives a much more adversely
weighted view of England than when he had thought he was weighting
the account in the other direction in Brobdingnag. He now prejudges
everything he reveals.[9] Only the evil aspects of every subject are mentioned: Lawyers are "bred up from their Youth in the Art of proving by
Words multiplied for the Purpose, that *White* is *Black,* and *Black* is
White." (p. 232) Judges are "picked out from the most dextrous Lawyers who are grown old or lazy: And having been byassed all their Lives
against Truth and Equity, lie under such a fatal Necessity of favouring
Fraud, Perjury and Oppression; that I have known some of them to have

9. I am indebted in the treatment of Gulliver's prejudices to H. D. Kelling, *"Gulliver's
Travels: A Comedy of Humours," University of Toronto Quarterly, 21* (1952), 362–75.

refused a large Bribe from the Side where Justice lay, rather then injure
the *Faculty,* by doing any thing unbecoming their Nature or their Office."
(p. 233) And so it is with all sorts and conditions of men as Gulliver
surveys them supposedly with detached candor. The application which
the horse makes of the analogy with the Yahoos is actually already made
in Gulliver's account since Gulliver is seeing all Europeans as Yahoos.
But besides this basic obliquity in presentation, which far exceeds that of
the irony of Gulliver's unwitting betrayal of human corruption in Book
II, there is great range within the account in the degree of allegory. There
is literal statement: "BUT, besides real Diseases, we are subject to many
that are only imaginary, for which the Physicians have invented imaginary Cures; these have their several Names, and so have the Drugs
that are proper for them; and with these our Female *Yahoos* are always
infested." (p. 238) Indeed the whole account of disease and medicine is
perfectly straightforward. But in the account of the causes of war, there
is great variation of management. Gulliver begins with a statement of
human quarrelsomeness in which the specific references are easily assign-
able:

> Difference in Opinions hath cost many Millions of Lives: For Instance,
> whether *Flesh* be *Bread,* or *Bread* be *Flesh:* Whether the Juice of a
> certain *Berry* be *Blood* or *Wine:* Whether *Whistling* be a Vice or a
> Virtue: Whether it be better to *kiss a Post,* or throw it into the Fire:
> What is the best Colour for a *Coat,* whether *Black, White, Red,* or
> *Grey;* and whether it should be *long* or *short, narrow* or *wide, dirty* or
> *clean;* with many more.

But he concludes the paragraph with a generalization:

> Neither are any Wars so furious and bloody, or of so long Continuance,
> as those occasioned by Difference in Opinion, especially if it be in
> things indifferent.

Then in the next paragraph, where the subject is greed as a source of war,
he abandons specific reference entirely and uses general statement with
irony to enforce the point:

> SOMETIMES the Quarrel between two Princes is to decide which of
> them shall dispossess a Third of his Dominions, where neither of them
> pretend to any Right. Sometimes one Prince quarreleth with another,
> for fear the other should quarrel with him. Sometimes a War is en-
> tered upon, because the Enemy is too *strong,* and sometimes because
> he is too *weak.* Sometimes our Neighbours *want* the *Things* which we
> *have,* or *have* the Things which we want; and we both fight, till they
> take ours or give us theirs. It is a very justifiable Cause of War to in-
> vade a Country after the People have been wasted by Famine, destroyed

by Pestilence, or embroiled by Factions amongst themselves. It is justifiable to enter into a War against our nearest Ally, when one of his Towns lies convenient for us, or a Territory of Land, that would render our Dominions round and compact. If a Prince send Forces into a Nation, where the People are poor and ignorant, he may lawfully put half of them to Death, and make Slaves of the rest, in order to civilize and reduce them from their barbarous Way of Living. It is a very kindly, honourable, and frequent Practice, when one Prince desires the Assistance of another to secure him against an Invasion, that the Assistant, when he hath driven out the Invader, should seize on the Dominions himself, and kill, imprison or banish the Prince he came to relieve. Allyance by Blood or Marriage, is a sufficient Cause of War between Princes; and the nearer the Kindred is, the greater is their Disposition to quarrel: *Poor* Nations are *hungry,* and *rich* Nations are *proud;* and Pride and Hunger will ever be at Variance. For these Reasons, the Trade of a *Soldier* is held the most honourable of all others: Because a *Soldier* is a *Yahoo* hired to kill in cold Blood as many of his own Species, who have never offended him, as possibly he can. (pp. 230–1)

This is in a very different vein from the story of the combat between Lilliput and Blefuscu, which carries the same implications; but it is no less packed and no less effective. Obviously it is not all allegory, though allegory shades very easily into irony of which there is full measure. Allegory itself is often a degree of irony. Or put the other way around, the irony here becomes an extension of allegory. Gulliver's analysis of war the more effectively illustrates Swift's skillful mixture of methods because it comes from a long disquisition where boredom from sameness of manner is the particular danger to be avoided.

One of the most complex of Swift's departures from the allegorical scheme is in the handling of Gulliver's own character. In a measure Gulliver must remain outside the allegory if our enlightenment is to come through his. His meditations on the shifted perspective at the beginning of Book ii, for instance, are the clues by which the whole sojourn in Brobdingnag is to be interpreted. And so in the other books, he is in part conveying Swift's attitude directly: the Lilliputians are "diminutive mortals"; the inhabitants of Laputa and Balnibarbi do contrive their houses ill; the Yahoos are the most "disagreeable" of animals. But Gulliver is also partly a comic figure who lacks perception. Clearly Swift does not intend him as a wholly reliable interpreter either in his initial failure to make any judgment at all or in the final state of disillusion in which he completely misjudges everything human. The necessity of a double interpretation of Gulliver's attitude makes constant demands on the reader. There is a relatively simple seeing beyond him in his failure to interpret the ridiculousness of Lilliputian pride. He lives up to the implications of gull in his name in his uncritical recording of the grandeur of the emperor's height and the bravery with which the monarch stands his ground at the shooting off of Gulliver's pistol. One of the most striking instances of his adoption of the Lilliputian point of view comes in the midst of the episode in which he demonstrates his immensely superior size by his way of putting out the fire in the queen's palace. He says complacently in speaking of the Lilliputian wine, Glimigrim: "the *Blefuscudians* call it *Flumec,* but ours is esteemed the better Sort." (p. 40) For the reader, the naïveté of Gulliver in Lilliput simply adds to the pleasure of discovering the meaning of the allegory for himself.

The situation in Brobdingnag is more complex. It is more natural that Gulliver should adopt the point of view of the Brobdingnagians since he is completely in their power. At the same time he is acutely conscious of the indignities he must suffer and feels that he would "rather have died than undergone the Disgrace of leaving a Posterity to be kept in Cages like tame Canary Birds." (p. 123) The scale itself, with its exact proportioning of Gulliver's size to the farmer's by the ratio of the Lilliputians' to his, immediately multiplies (one might almost say in the degree of twelve times twelve) the impression of man's insignificance and weakness already set up in Book I. It is not only that Gulliver has shifted from giant among pigmies to pigmy among giants. Within the compass of Book II, there is a double perspective: the giants show man's defects enlarged at the same time that Gulliver reveals human littleness. Disgust at man's physical being comes from the magnified stature, and scorn of his folly as well. The foolishness of parents seems very foolish indeed in the farmer's wife's indulgence of her baby's desire to have Gulliver for a plaything. What is dismissed as naughtiness in human boys seems cruelty when the giant farmer's son holds Gulliver high in the air by the legs and the mischievous schoolboy aims the hazel nut at his head. The silly fears of women are shown as peculiarly silly when the giantess screams at the sight of Gulliver. The explanation of the presence of the militia magnifies Swift's old theme of contests and dissensions in the state. Even the queen is susceptible to flattery, and the incapacity of man to bear derision is enforced by the ludicrousness of the picture of the farmer's visitor who peers at Gulliver as well as by his vindictiveness over being laughed at. The farmer enlarges the notion of everyday callousness in what Glumdalclitch says of the fate of her lamb as well as in his treatment of Gulliver. Yet through all the holding up of human defect to view through enlargement, human insignificance is steadily before us in Gulliver's littleness. He is first the pet of a child nurse, who dresses and undresses him as she has done her doll and puts him to bed in her doll cradle; then he becomes the plaything of the court. The impact of all this is intensified because it is combined with the memory of Lilliput. Swift reminds the reader at intervals of the early impression by Gulliver's own reflections upon relativity and upon the dishonorableness of his present state. In Book I he indulges in some reflections upon courts and princes, but almost none upon his human condition. The only hint in Book I of the kind of awareness that grows upon him in Book II is in the sixth chapter, where he says: "the Emperor thought it monstrous in me to offer, as a Defence, the greatest Aggravation of the Crime: And truly, I had little to say in Return, farther than the common Answer, that different Nations had different Customs; for, I confess, I was heartily ashamed." (p. 42) But this meditation seems as uncharacteristic as does the whole of the sixth chapter. In Book II, on the other hand, Gulliver's somber reflections begin almost at once. It is in the first chapter that he says: "In this terrible agitation of Mind I could not forbear thinking of *Lilliput,* whose Inhabitants looked upon me as the greatest Prodigy that ever appeared in the World; . . . Undoubtedly Philosophers are in the Right when they tell us, that nothing is great or little otherwise than by Comparison." (pp. 70–1) And the degrading comparisons of the kinds of small animals that come to Gulliver's mind to explain what he feels is the Brobdingnagian attitude to him do almost as much to drive home the conception as does his insignificant size. But while we share Gulliver's distress, we also partly share the Brobdingnagian amusement at him. The scenes themselves are funny when the farmer places him on the ground "upon all four" or when he stumbles against the crust or is imprisoned in the marrow bone; and Gulliver makes himself more absurd than he needs to be by trying to act big among this race of giants. His folly in engaging in feats of strength makes him ridiculous in more than size.

This mixed relation of Gulliver to the allegory sharpens the effect of the ridiculous in the first voyage, and is used in the second as one of the central means of redoubling the comic impression. Gulliver's power of exact literal statement of what he sees, and his failure to perceive many implications of what he states make him at once instrument and object of the satire. Throughout the first two books the reader is conscious of Gulliver in both functions and adapts his own point of view according to his own pride. In Book III, the attitude of Gulliver wavers between criticism in Swift's voice: "I never knew a Soil so unhappily cultivated, Houses so ill contrived and so ruinous, or a People whose Countenances and Habit expressed so much Misery and Want" (p. 159) and the sort of naïve plain citizen's judgment which finds in the only proposals of wisdom and morality in the School of Political Projectors the proof that the professors are "wholly out of their Senses." (p. 171) But in the third voyage, Swift does not leave any question about when he is using Gulliver to give his own actual views and when an ironic reversal of them. In the fourth voyage, however, not only is there a dissociation of one of Gulliver's uses from the other; but one holds sway for the first nine chapters, and then the other completely takes over.[1] At first the allegorical representation of man's uncontrolled passion and animality in the Yahoos is set over against the allegorical representation of the passionless following of Reason and Nature in the horses. Gulliver is outside the pattern of idea, though he records his admiration for the one extreme and his revulsion from the other. Since the loathsome physical details in the concrete representation of the Yahoos so powerfully reinforce the revelation of their depravity, the sense of evil conveyed by them is overwhelming. Because we look for an expression of the standard of judgment in satire, and because the Houyhnhnms are sharply contrasted with the Yahoos, we expect to find in them such a standard. But it is not Swift's satiric habit to give an unequivocal statement to his positive pattern; nor does he do so here. He makes perfectly clear when he takes Gulliver back into the allegoric scheme and shows him as a type, possessed by an obsession, that the Houyhnhnms do not represent a human ideal. Gulliver's adoption of the horses' gait and voice is more absurd than his attempts to show the court of Brobdingnag how strong he is. If the horses themselves are slightly ridiculous, Gulliver is more so when in his desire to be "reasonable," he tries to act like a horse. Swift makes ludicrous such pictures as that of the horses sitting on their haunches to dine from their "Mangers . . . placed circular in the Middle of the Room" (p. 215) or the white mare threading a needle held between the pastern and hoof of her forefeet; but he makes Gulliver still more "unnatural" in his preferring the company of his two young Stone-Horses to that of his wife and children. Swift plainly shows in Gulliver that the attempt to live by inhuman standards of reason and benevolence produces madness and ruthlessness. The gross rudeness to the kind and forbearing Don Pedro, who does not (like his men and the earlier Captains John Biddel and Thomas Wilcocks) assume that Gulliver is mad but tries to help him return to a normal life, and the monstrous cruelty to his wife are the demonstration of his pathological state. He is brought fully back into the allegory as the representation of the foolish pride of a human attempt to live by reason alone. It is characteristic of Swift's complexity of approach that the climax of his indictment of human pride comes from the victim of the most extreme degree of it. It is the Gulliver who with sublime pride entreats "those who have any Tincture of this absurd Vice, that they will not presume to appear in [his] Sight" (p. 280) who has just delivered the final denunciation of this central human weakness:

I am not in the least provoked at the Sight of a Lawyer, a Pick-pocket, a Colonel, a Fool, a Lord, a Gamester, a Politician, a Whoremunger, a Physician, an Evidence, a Suborner, an Attorney, a Traytor, or the

1. The shift in the allegory corresponds exactly to the turn from corrosive to comic satire pointed out by John F. Ross in "The Final Comedy of Lemuel Gulliver," *Studies in the Comic, University of California Publications in English, 8* (1941), 175–96.

like: This is all according to the due Course of Things: But, when I behold a Lump of Deformity, and Diseases both in Body and Mind, smitten with *Pride,* it immediately breaks all the Measures of my Patience; neither shall I be ever able to comprehend how such an Animal and such a Vice could tally together.

This arraignment gains ironic emphasis because Gulliver is proving, in his own failure to perceive that he comes under his own condemnation, the universal sway of pride. Yet in spite of the many recent criticisms that insist on the clarity with which Swift has shown that he does not intend the Houyhnhnms as a human ideal, it is still true that many readers retain the view which held sway in 19th-century criticism that Swift in Book IV is Gulliver and is holding up the horses as an ideal, writing in despair, or as W. B. C. Watkin would have it,[2] writing Gulliver's tragedy. The reason, I think, for the resistance to the view that Gulliver's worship of the horses is an aberration is the too sudden shift in the use Swift makes of his relation to the allegory. He has left Gulliver outside the allegory for so long and has compelled such complete participation in Gulliver's attitude toward the Yahoos that the reader is inclined to adopt his view of the Houyhnhnms too, or at least to think that Swift intends this, however unattractive the cool detachment of the horses seems. Swift supplies the clue to his intention exactly in making the horses seem incomplete in their absence of affection and learning, of humanity itself; but since he seems to give through Gulliver his own view of the Yahoos, he suggests that he shares Gulliver's admiration for the horses. The demonstration of the disastrous effect of this admiration on Gulliver when he is taken back into the allegorical pattern comes too late to serve Swift's artistic purpose with complete success.

The consideration of the range in Swift's handling of departures from the allegorical scheme, which in their total effect are a source of enrichment, brings a return to the related question about consistency in management of levels of meaning. In Books II and IV, there are very few suggestions of particular events. Swift is content to let the allegory represent the larger truths of man's nature without at the same time representing particular men. In the first and third books, however, he is experimenting with the sort of allegory which through its particulars at once depicts universals and another set of particulars. In these two books Swift uses the same sort of freedom in shifting from details which carry two levels of meaning beyond the surface to those which carry only one that he uses throughout in departures from the allegorical scheme. In Book I the shifts make a reciprocal enhancement of effect. The particular absurdity of Whig and Tory quarrels and the larger folly of faction itself are epitomized in the quarrels of high and low heels. But this account,

2. *Perilous Balance* (Princeton, 1939), pp. 4–6.

which gives a double representation of human self-importance, gains from the pictures of human pettiness and pride which have no specific reference to England and also contributes to the total impression of human absurdity. It is as enlightening about 20th-century political parties as about Whigs and Tories. And so throughout the first book. Events in England and the relations between England and France furnish a pleasing narrative framework; but the reader is not disturbed if the inhabitants of Lilliput and Blefuscu act much of the time simply as human beings rather than specifically as Englishmen and Frenchmen. In Book III, however, which has no such narrative scheme, it is often hard to tell when there is a specific reference beyond the mockery of theoretical speculation in the management of affairs. The moment of suspense that intensifies the force and pleasure with which the mind leaps into understanding becomes an appreciable period of puzzling out references. The problems seem too thorny and the pleasure of solving them too long delayed. In Book I, we see that Flimnap is Walpole (or some specific first minister) as soon as we see the larger mockery of human folly in the sentence: *"Flimnap,* the Treasurer, is allowed to cut a Caper on the strait Rope, at least an Inch higher than any other Lord in the whole Empire." (p. 22) The mockery of Flimnap's skill in acrobatic feats and of maneuvering for place have a reciprocal intensification. But in the episode of the mill in Book III, while the ridicule of speculative schemes is at once apparent, we are tantalized by the specific applications. The arguments of scholars over the events signified by this and other references are indicative of an artistic defect which mars the whole voyage. If we take the reference to contemporary life as the first level of meaning, the distance to an interpretation of it in which we can feel any confidence is so great that we are discouraged before we reach the second and third levels of comment on theorizing in the management of public economy and on theorizing as such. Thus the deeper significance is almost lost. The artistic weakness is fundamental and has nothing to do with the passage of time, which causes no difficulty in the equally contemporary references of Book I. In the Voyage to Lilliput, Swift so early and so clearly establishes both levels of his allegorical scheme under the surface of an easily grasped narrative which carries both, that the movement back and forth between details which carry only general reference and those which carry specific ones as well adds to the pleasure in the allegory. In the third voyage, he not only works without an appealing narrative; he also waits until he has firmly (and apparently exclusively) established theorizing in general as the meaning behind the allegory before he intrudes details that must be applied to particular events. Thus the reader is left wondering if he has missed some of the meaning of the allegory .The insecurity in the management of the levels of implications has much to do with the comparative lack of success in the third voyage. Swift's control is surer in

Book I than in Book III in handling the levels of his allegory as in other aspects of his art.

The freedom with which Swift injects nonallegorical elements into the narrative and moves about among levels of allegorical intention are indications of the richness and complexity of his handling of allegory which is borne out in another way. There is great range in the various representations of ideas that are repeated from book to book. Perhaps the most insistently presented is the condemnation of war and rapaciousness in conquest, which runs from the Lilliputian desire to reduce Blefuscu to servitude, through the Laputan king's being restrained in punishing the kingdoms which lie beneath his sway only by the self-interest of the nobles whose own estates are below the flying island, to the Yahoos' quarreling among five to possess all of food sufficient for fifty or fighting battles "without any visible Cause" (p. 244), with the straightforward denunciations of the King of Brobdingnag and Gulliver's Houyhnhnm master added for good measure. Each of the representations gains something from all the others. Swift uses the same sort of reduplication of other ideas. The ruthlessness of kingly power is ironically presented in Lilliput in the insistence on the great lenity of the articles of impeachment. Gulliver remarks: "IT was a Custom introduced by this Prince and his Ministry, (very different, as I have been assured, from the Practices of former Times) that after the Court had decreed any cruel Execution, either to gratify the Monarch's Resentment, or the Malice of a Favourite; the Emperor always made a Speech to his whole Council, expressing his *great Lenity and Tenderness, as Qualities known and confessed by all the World.*" (p. 56) The abuse of kingly power under the guise of lenity is differently allegorized in Book III when the King of Luggnagg graciously forgives the page who has caused the death of a young lord by neglecting to see to the washing of the poison from the floor where all who approach his majesty must lick the dust. This callousness on the part of rulers is reflected in the utter failure of all the people Gulliver visits to see anything from his point of view. Since they are not wholly human beings, it is not remarkable that they fail to perceive his human reactions; and his docility in accepting the attitudes of the lands he visits is, to be sure, part of Swift's means of projecting these attitudes. But the utter unawareness of most of Gulliver's hosts that he too has a sense of himself repeatedly gives allegorical expression to the unkindness that comes from lack of imagination. The Lilliputians discuss what disposition to make of the Man-mountain with as little regard for any interest but their own as the farmer who owns the animated toy in Brobdingnag displays in working him to exhaustion and then selling him before being cheated by death. Even the assembly of horses bid his Houyhnhnm master to dismiss Gulliver with no thought except to rid their own land of an undesirable inhabitant. Closely allied to the inability or unwillingness to consider

Gulliver's feelings are the ignorant surmises as to his nature. Swift alle-gorizes in all except the third voyage, where the people are too wrapped up in their own theorizing to be curious about a stranger, the human propensity to give plausible explanations to what the explainers do not understand. The conclusions of the committee who examine Gulliver's pockets in Lilliput and the statement of the king's experts in Brobding-nag are no more farfetched than the complacent speculations of the Houyhnhnms. Swift's censure of the willingness to pass unwarranted judgments is paralleled by the use of curiosity about laws and customs as a criterion of intelligence. The wise King of Brobdingnag hears Gulliver in five audiences before he begins to raise objections; and his horse master not only examines Gulliver, but takes him into company to be questioned by others. The King of Laputa, on the other hand, does not care for Gulliver's conversation: "His Majesty discovered not the least Curiosity to enquire into the Laws, Government, History, Religion, or Manners of the Countries where I had been; but confined his Questions to the State of Mathematics, and received the Account I gave him, with great Contempt and Indifference, though often roused by his *Flapper* on each Side." (p. 150) And the Struldbrugs, "although they were told that I was a great Traveller, and had seen all the World, . . . had not the least Curiosity to ask me a Question." (p. 197) Underneath Swift's laughter at these betrayals of Gulliver's own desire to show off his knowledge, there is a real indictment of those who do not care to learn. One more example may be mentioned to show how Swift circles round and round a subject before he lets it drop. The idea of man's having declined from an earlier and better state is reiterated in all four books with varying degrees of allegorical indirection. The parenthesis in Gulliver's comment on the lenity of the King of Lilliput is one indication of it. His apology for the utopian sixth chapter of Book 1 is another: it describes "the original Institutions, and not the most scandalous Corruptions into which these People are fallen by the degenerate Nature of Man." (p. 44) The King of Brobdingnag observes that the original institutions of England "might have been tolerable; but these half erased and the rest wholly blurred and blotted by Corruptions." (p. 116) The book of morality which Gulliver reads in Brobdingnag declared that "Nature was degenerated in these latter declining Ages of the World, and could now produce only small abortive Births in Comparison of those in ancient Times." (p. 121) Al-though Gulliver somewhat uneasily laughs at the giants' repining over physical decline, he himself makes the same reflection in Glubdubdrib: "As every Person called up made exactly the same Appearance he had done in the World, it gave me melancholy Reflections to observe how much the Race of human Kind was degenerate among us, within these Hundred Years past. How the Pox under all its Consequences and De-nominations had altered every Lineament of an *English* Countenance;

shortened the Size of Bodies, unbraced the Nerves, relaxed the Sinews and Muscles, introduced a sallow Complexion, and rendered the Flesh loose and *rancid*." (p. 185) The same theme appears in Book IV as one theory of the origin of the Yahoos which "affirmed, that the two Yahoos said to be first seen among them, had been driven thither over the Sea; . . . and degenerating by Degrees, became in Process of Time, much more savage than those of their own Species in the Country from whence these two Originals came." (p. 256) All of the references to a given topic enforce each other. Every time Swift returns to a subject, he gives it a different dress and reveals a slightly different implication of idea. This richness of allegorical revelation makes a thickness of texture in the image which establishes the importance of the idea to be conveyed. The way Swift varies the representation of his recurrent themes is one of the most emphatic proofs of his skill in satiric allegory.

In large measure, the possibility of this sort of reciprocal enrichment of one allegorical representation of an idea by another grows out of the basic structure of the work in four voyages. One of the ways Swift surpasses his predecessors in the use of the imaginary journey for comment on the real world is in using for his allegory a succession of journeys which operate upon each other. The time element itself and the returns to the world of humanity are important in the progress of Gulliver's disillusionment; and the impression of development marks the whole treatment of satiric ideas. Swift depends upon the preceding voyages in the management of the allegory in each one after the first. This is a matter not just of such direct use of an earlier voyage as Gulliver's reflections in Brobdingnag on Lilliputian scale. It is even more important in the allegorical concepts of the successive voyages. The beings who inhabit the allegorical worlds that Gulliver visits are progressively less human from voyage to voyage. This progression is another demonstration of Swift's power to win belief and then gradually inject what gives purpose to his fiction. Gulliver and the reader alike are led by almost imperceptible degrees through the increasing isolation of human traits in the first three books to the complete abstractions of the fourth, where the nonhuman quality of entire absence of propensity to evil is given the nonhuman form of the horse. Gulliver's "insatiable Desire" for travel does more than make plausible the mere fact of his taking four journeys. It becomes itself a part of the intensification as he records it with increasing impression of mania at the beginning of each voyage. He has started life with the assumption that he would travel and has made various voyages, though the one which takes him to Lilliput he embarks on without enthusiasm simply because of an "advantageous Offer." (p. 4) But the voyage to Brobdingnag begins with a feeling of ill omen: "HAVING been condemned by Nature and Fortune to an active and restless Life." (p. 67) There is more of apology in his explanation of why he sets out a third time: "the Thirst I had of seeing the World, notwithstanding my past Misfortunes, continuing as violent as ever." (pp. 137–8) And with the clarity of hindsight he perceives the folly of his having embarked on a fourth voyage: "I CONTINUED at home with my Wife and Children about five Months in a very happy Condition, if I could have learned the Lesson of knowing when I was well. I left my poor Wife big with Child, and accepted an advantageous Offer made me to be Captain of the *Adventure*." (p. 205) The stranger the beings he encounters are, the more impossible it is for him to readjust himself and be content with human life, until he is finally completely unfitted for it and thinks of his "poor Wife" as an "odious Animal" whom he can tolerate no nearer to him than the opposite end of the table. Conversely, the more foolhardy and intense his desire for travel grows, the stronger the preparation for the increasing strangeness of the lands he visits. It is impossible to consider any of the later voyages without reference to the ones which have gone before. The narrative scheme by the very device which makes possible the rich variety in the allegorical treatment of ideas compels the reader to view all the books together as an artistic whole. In choosing such an organization for his allegory, Swift provides at once for its range and its integration as an organic unity. Within the frame of this perfectly chosen plan, he is able to make clear very early that his fiction is an allegory carrying satiric ideas and then to proceed to an ever more intensely allegorical presentation of his increasingly searching satire.

6

Satiric Journeys II: Erewhon

"Sometimes to passe the Ocean we would faine
Sometimes to other worlds."
SAMUEL DANIEL

THE VICTORIAN age produced no more self-confident work than Butler's high-hearted mocking of all Victorian complacencies in *Erewhon*. The youthful zest and exuberance of the writer carry the reader along as the mind of the satirist sweeps over the subjects of education, religion, law, convention, health, evolution, and technology—to mention only major items in his survey. The vitality does not flag even in the flatly labeled "Book of the Machines." There is something wistful about the remark with which the older Butler concludes the preface to *Erewhon Revisited: "Nevertheless, though in literary workmanship I do not doubt that this last-named book is an improvement on the first, I shall be agreeably surprised if I am not told that 'Erewhon,' with all its faults, is the better reading of the two."* [1] One of the reasons why the earlier book is better reading is the sheer energy which is communicated in the brisk, matter-of-fact beginning and propels the reader straight through to the end.

The opening chapters establish at once the impression that what is being given is a true narrative of exploration. This effect is due partly to the engaging frankness of manner, but also partly to the feeling of authenticity of detail which comes from the fact that the details are actually authentic. The first four chapters of *Erewhon* produce the same sort of response as *A First Year in Canterbury Settlement,* written while Butler was pioneering in New Zealand as letters describing his adventures to his family and published by his father. In the preface to the revised edition of *Erewhon* published with *Erewhon Revisited,* Butler remarks merely *"that the opening chapters of 'Erewhon' were also drawn from the Upper Rangitata district, with such modifications as I found convenient."* (p. xi) But R. A. Streatfield in his introduction to *A First Year in Canterbury Settlement* quotes Butler's letter of 1889 to Alfred Marks, who

---

1. *Erewhon and Erewhon Revisited* (Modern Library ed.), p. xv. All references are to this edition unless otherwise indicated.

had purchased a copy of the then already rare first book of the author: "I stole a passage or two from it for *Erewhon*." [2] The connection is closer even than this acknowledgement reveals, for not only are there passages such as the waking to find the last night's tea leaves frozen in the pannikins, the explanation of knowing that the sheep are all right because

> you will soon have a large number of sheep with whom you are personally acquainted, and who have, from time to time, forced themselves upon your attention either by peculiar beauty or peculiar ugliness, or by having certain marks upon them. You will have a black sheep or two, and probably a long-tailed one or two, and a sheep with only one eye, and another with a wart on its nose, and so forth. These will be your marked sheep, and if you find all of them you may be satisfied that the rest are safe also,

and the description of the woolshed as a "roomy covered building, with a large central space, and an aisle-like partition on each side," [3] which appear slightly modified in *Erewhon;* but the whole sense of the beauty of the country and the hazard and excitement of moving about among its rivers with their rushing waters and beds of large shingle, its gorges and precipitous mountains and strange valleys, is conveyed in the same way. The style, even though the tamperings of Butler's father may have removed some of what Streatfield calls the "cocksureness" of the earlier work, has in both books the same sort of matter-of-fact dispatch and energy that conveys the very ring of truth so useful to the writer whose design is to give credibility to a fantastic world. The terrifying journey made by the hero of *Erewhon* after Chowbook deserts him is as convincing in the sensation of icy waters and perilous rocks as is the early essay "Crossing the Rangitata," which Streatfield published in its original form as an example of Butler's "fresh and spirited . . . descriptions of his adventures" ungroomed by his father's editing. The stamp of truth is equally upon both. How careful Butler was to keep to what his eye had actually observed and his body felt is revealed in his note on

THE GEOGRAPHY OF EREWHON

Up as far as the top of the pass where the statues are keeps to the actual geography of the upper Rangitata district except that I have doubled the gorge. There was no gorge up above my place . . . and I wanted one, so I took the gorge some ten or a dozen miles lower down and repeated it, and then came upon my own country again, but made it bare of grass and useless instead of (as it actually was) excellent country. Baker and I went up the last saddle we tried, and

2. *The Shrewsbury Edition of the Works of Samuel Butler,* ed. H. F. Jones and A. T. Bartholomew (London, 1923), *i*, xi.
3. Ibid., pp. 111, 174, and 175.

thought it was a pass to the West Coast, but found it looked down on to the headwaters of the Rakaia: however we saw a true pass opposite, just as I have described in *Erewhon* only that there were no clouds, and we never went straight down as I said I did, but took two days going round by lake Heron. And there is no lake at the top of the true pass. This is the pass which in consequence of our report Whitcombe was sent over and got drowned on the other side. We went up to the top of the pass, but found it too rough to go down without more help than we had. I rather think I have told this in my New Zealand book, but am so much ashamed of that book that I dare not look to see. I don't mean to say that the later books are much better, still they are better.

They shew a lot of stones on the Hokitika pass, so Mr Slade told me, which they call mine, and say I intended them in *Erewhon*. I never saw them, and knew nothing about them.[4]

Thus meticulous is Butler about details of the geography of real far away places when he is about to plunge the reader into a world that exists only in his mind as an upside down picture of the England near at hand. The impression of his telling about an actual adventure for the sheer fun of describing it, as he had recounted those in *A First Year in Canterbury Settlement,* is so successfully created that once Higgs (as he may be called for convenience, though Butler does not give him this name until *Erewhon Revisited*) has reached the strange land beyond the statues, we are interested simply in connecting his observations with the implications about our own world. Butler does not have to bother any more about winning acceptance of the outward story as true.

The tremendous climax of the statues with their Handelian music marks the entrance to a new world. The shift from what seems pure adventure narrative to what is obviously an allegorical mockery of one after another of the shibboleths of Victorian society may be too abrupt for artistic smoothness; but it would be a finicky reader indeed who would object to the rush with which Butler pushes on from the excitement of outward happening to the excitement of ideas. From the time that the shepherd girls discover the stranger asleep under the tree, there is hardly any interest in action until the tale of the escape with Arowhena returns in the next to the last chapter to the feeling of an adventure story. Butler points this out rather apologetically in the preface to the revised edition published with *Erewhon Revisited* in 1901: *"There is no central idea underlying 'Erewhon,' whereas the attempt to realize the effect of a single supposed great miracle dominates the whole of its successor. In 'Erewhon' there was hardly any story, and little attempt to give life and individuality to the characters; I hope that in 'Erewhon Revisited' both these defects*

---

4. *Samuel Butler's Notebooks, Selections,* ed. Geoffrey Keynes and Brian Hill (London, 1951), pp. 143–4.

have been in great measure avoided. 'Erewhon' was not an organic whole, 'Erewhon Revisited' may fairly claim to be one." (p. xv) Then follows the rather puzzled and melancholy statement already quoted about *Erewhon's* being, nevertheless, the better reading. It is surprising that Butler does not seem to realize that he has just explained the superiority of the earlier book. In *Erewhon Revisited* he keeps the reader so agitated throughout about the fate of Higgs that the absorption of the people in their false religion holds interest almost solely as the source of his danger rather than as a comment on the miraculous in religion. It is exactly in giving the later book so engrossing a plot and characters whose fate seems the central concern that he wrecks it as satiric allegory. When the allegorical comment is thrust upon attention, it seems an intrusion in what has been progressing simply as an adventure novel.

Erewhon, on the other hand, for all its range of subjects, has a clearcut unity of conception. The allegorical point of view is sustained and keeps attention fixed on the satire. The reader knows all the time that he is at once in Erewhon, in England, and in the realm of ideas in Butler's mind. In his Notebooks there is the revealing comment on IMAGINARY COUNTRIES: "Why should we be at such pains to describe adventurous journeys to these? Surely we have not far to go before we find them. They are like the Kingdom of Heaven—'within us.' " [5] We are traveling over the country of Butler's attitudes; and the nimbleness with which we are required to leap from one to another is an indication of the variety of the country. It is this feeling that the really important world is the one in Butler's mind which makes the curious complexity and interest (and sometimes mere perversity) of the relation between the worlds of England and Erewhon. Something of the point of view is indicated by the witticism in Butler's rather flippant essay "Quis Desiderio . . . ?": "Besides, I have a great respect for my namesake, and always say that if *Erewhon* had been a racehorse it would have been got by *Hudibras* out of *Analogy*. Someone said this to me many years ago, and I felt so much flattered that I have been repeating the remark as my own ever since." [6]

Sometimes Butler seems to be standing on his head for the mere fun of kicking his heels in the air. The whole to-do over the Erewhonians as the ten lost tribes of Israel appears irrelevant to anything else Butler is mocking until he presents the barbarity of Higgs's scheme for converting them in the last chapter and quotes beside it the following extract from the *Times:*

POLYNESIANS IN QUEENSLAND.—The Marquis of Normanby, the new Governor of Queensland, has completed his inspection of the

5. Ibid., p. 174.
6. *Selected Essays by Samuel Butler,* ed. H. F. Jones (London, 1930), p. 113.

northern districts of the colony. It is stated that at Mackay, one of
the best sugar-growing districts, his Excellency saw a good deal of the
Polynesians. In the course of a speech to those who entertained him
there, the Marquis said:—'I have been told that the means by which
Polynesians were obtained were not legitimate, but I have failed to
perceive this, in so far at least as Queensland is concerned; and, if one
can judge by the countenances and manners of the Polynesians, they
experience no regret at their position.' But his Excellency pointed out
the advantage of giving them religious instruction. It would tend to
set at rest an uneasy feeling which at present existed in the country
to know that they were inclined to retain the Polynesians, and teach
them religion. (pp. 305–6)

The absence of cats and tobacco and the diatonic scale is never related
to any meaning and seems purely capricious. The reversal of names to fit
the derivation of Erewhon from nowhere is carried beyond the simple
Yram and Senoj Nosnibor and Thims to the more complicated Arowhena, with its suggestion of anywhere and anywhen and the universality
of falling in love; but it is not consistent, for some of the names like
Zulora and Mahaina are merely concocted of random syllables. The process of reversal of spelling obviously continued to amuse Butler, for he
adds in the revised version in the chapter on the Colleges of Unreason the
phrase: "a city whose Erewhonian name is so cacophonous that I refrain
from giving it" (p. 219), which would certainly be true of either Drofxo
or Egdirbmac. The Notebooks show his pleasure in the sheer surprise of
reversing what is accepted, especially on Biblical authority, as the following entries illustrate:

Hating
with a hatred passing the hate of women.

'WOE UNTO YOU WHEN ALL MEN SPEAK WELL OF YOU'
Yes, and 'Woe unto you when you speak well of all men.'

The Lilies Say
'Consider the Solomons in all their glory; they toil not neither do
they spin, yet verily I say unto you that not a lily among you is
arrayed like one of these.' [7]

This last apparently pleased him so much that he included it in the chapter on "The Rights of Vegetables," which he added to the revised edition
of *Erewhon*. Yet even so trivial a matter is related to the essential point
of view, for while Butler is constantly announcing that the Erewhonians
have distorted notions, he makes these notions sometimes parallel the
English ideas he is ridiculing and sometimes reverse them. Occasionally

7. *Notebooks*, pp. 265, 260, and 176.

he lets the reader relax with what seems a fairly simple parallel of some familiar attitude, as when he writes of the Erewhonian straighteners, or doctors of morals : "they are always able to tell a man what is the matter with him as soon as they have heard his story, and their familiarity with the long names assures him that they thoroughly understand his case." (p. 93) Even here the irony at the expense of doctors involves some comment on the moral straighteners of our own world, though Butler could hardly have foreseen its application to psychiatry. Often the same comment on Erewhon must be applied both by parallel and by reversal, or by a more complicated readjustment of viewpoint. This is partly what makes the satire cut so incisively in several directions. The judge's summing up against the prisoner accused of "the great crime of laboring under pulmonary consumption," (p. 106) has been described as creating a feeling of "insoluble dilemma," an anxiety "deeper than the indignation which it is called upon to stimulate." [8] It is the element of insoluble dilemma which gives substance to *Erewhon* and makes it deeply disturbing. It is no mere *jeu d'esprit,* however sportively Butler treats his subjects. Since overearnestness is one of the qualities he is mocking, he is as careful not to seem earnest as is Oscar Wilde in *The Importance of Being Earnest;* but he is also like Wilde in having a serious comment to make, and he is the more successful of the two satirists in communicating a sense of disturbance by his reversals of values.

Butler goes with unflagging zest from one indictment of accepted standards of judgment to another. Perhaps the most pervasive sign of the "entire perversion of thought which exists among this extraordinary people" (p. 104) is the transposing of the European attitude toward disease and crime. The rich implications about the unreasonableness of actual treatment of both sorts of defect are explored in the greatest detail ; and though there has been a subtle shift since Butler's day in what seems topsy-turvy in the Erewhonian notions, there is still enough strangeness in them to make us take notice of what is really perverse in our own ways of looking at moral and physical disorders. Indeed, the movement, at least in theory, away from the vindictive to the restorative treatment of criminals probably owes something to Butler's influence ; and it is not too much to say that the Erewhonian belief in health as the cardinal virtue has made us at least more receptive than our grandparents were to the notions of psychosomatic medicine, though the praise or blame for the current cults which worship the idea of health with an Erewhonian ardor can hardly be given to Butler.

Since the conception runs through the whole book, there is a good deal of variety in its allegorical presentation. Butler begins it with the demonstration that the belief in health has worked well in Erewhon. The first impression Higgs has of the people is that of surpassing physical beauty

8. P. N. Furbank, *Samuel Butler* (Cambridge, 1948), pp. 9 and 8.

and well-being. He is "dazzled with [the] extreme beauty" (p. 46) of the girls who discover him; and he finds the group they bring to look at him just as charming: "Both the girls and the men were very dark in color, but not more so than the South Italians or Spaniards. The men wore no trousers, but were dressed nearly the same as the Arabs whom I have seen in Algeria. They were of the most magnificent presence, being no less strong and handsome than the women were beautiful; and not only this, but their expression was courteous and benign." (p. 46) The virtue of health, with its consequent beauty, is very generally practiced in Erewhon so that not many have to be punished for being ill. Yram is terribly angry with Higgs for having a cold and especially for being rude enough to speak to her about it; so he promptly recovers. This seems to be the general effect of the attitude, though most families have their concealed medicine chests, and there is the danger of the underground practice of medicine which must be constantly watched and severely put down by the authorities. It is the fact of the hero's having "more to glory in the flesh than in any other respect" (p. 47) and especially his having the singular merit of fair hair which keeps him from being punished for having a watch, almost as great a crime as a case of typhus. But though they value his fairness because of its rarity, Higgs thinks the dark-skinned Erewhonians the most beautiful people he has ever seen. The repeated comparison of them with Italians is a recommendation of them from Butler, to whom all associations with Italy were pleasant.

Like the comment on moral health through the presentation of physical well-being, Butler's use of physical distress as an allegory for moral defect is charged with irony. In spite of the devotion with which the belief in health is generally supported, some Erewhonians are wicked enough to be ill. In the town where Higgs is taken by his first captors, he is brought before the magistrate from a cell with two other people who are plainly "out of health." And from his own pleasant quarters, once he is put in Yram's custody, he hears the sounds of their groaning and coughing in another part of the prison as they work out the long term of confinement with hard labor to which the judge condemns them. The impressive trial of the consumptive is one of the vivid episodes of Higgs's sojourn at the metropolis. In the revision of the book to include the theory of misfortune of any sort as sin, Butler adds two other trials for various afflictions to the chapter now called "Some Erewhonian Trials" and thus weakens the allegory and the satire. In the original work, the trial of the consumptive stands alone as the grand demonstration of the Erewhonian idea of the enormity of ill health, even in the view of the culprit himself, who "acknowledged in a few scarcely audible words that he was justly punished, and that he had had a fair trial." (pp. 110–11) Besides the openly ill, whose diseases are so flagrant as to be beyond concealment, there are those like poor Mahaina, who must pretend to be addicted to drink in order to hide her indigestion. In fact, says Higgs of the Erewhonians, while Butler laughs through him at Europeans:

> In their eagerness to stamp out disease, these people overshot their mark; for people had become so clever at dissembling—they painted their faces with such consummate skill—they repaired the decay of time and the effects of mischance with such profound dissimulation— that it was really impossible to say whether any one was well or ill till after an intimate acquaintance of months or years. Even then the shrewdest were constantly mistaken in their judgments, and marriages were often contracted with most deplorable results, owing to the art with which infirmity had been concealed. (p. 135)

The relation of this comment to the moral world is pertinent enough by itself. Butler never makes the mistake of offering the interpretation. But he doubles the effect by insisting with a reiteration only less pervasive than that on the views of disease, on the corresponding view that crime or moral disorder of any sort is simply a distressing affliction, to be treated with sympathy and healed.

Again he lets the hero learn Erewhonian ideas partly from the response of the people to his own behavior. On his progress to the metropolis, he is beset with the attentions of the interested, kindly Erewhonians.

> They never once asked after my health, or even whether I was fatigued with my journey; but their first question was almost invariably an inquiry after my temper, the *naïveté* of which astonished me until I became used to it. One day, being tired and cold, and weary of saying the same thing over and over again, I turned a little brusquely on my questioner and said that I was exceedingly cross, and that I could hardly feel in a worse humor with myself and every one else than at that moment. To my surprise, I was met with the kindest expressions of condolence, and heard it buzzed about the room that I was in an ill temper; whereon people began to give me nice things to smell and to eat, which really did seem to have some temper-mending quality about them, for I soon felt pleased and was at once congratulated upon being better. (p. 79)

Higgs's naïve discovery that attention makes him feel better is highly characteristic of Butler's irony, which works in several directions at once. He allows the reader to smile at Higgs's simplicity, but not to arrive at his own meaning by a mere reversal of Higgs's.

Butler sustains the parallel with his treatment of Erewhonian ideas of illness by again arranging a progression and deepening of the allegorical and satiric effect. Just as in learning the Erewhonian views of health, the hero observes far more serious crimes than his own cold in the head, so he discovers that there are moral indispositions greater than his crossness which require more strenuous methods of cure. He has already had to adjust his mind to the fact that his host in the metropolis is to be a distinguished citizen who is just recovering from a serious case of embezzling. On the day of his arrival, he finds that Mr. Nosnibor is to receive the eleventh of the twelve floggings prescribed for his cure by the famous straightener called in to deal with his important case. "As the afternoon wore on many carriages drove up with callers to inquire how he had stood his flogging." (p. 99) But no one dreams of mentioning his physical health. Higgs observes: "On a subsequent occasion I was present at an interview between Mr. Nosnibor and the family straightener, who was considered competent to watch the completion of the cure. I was struck with the delicacy with which he avoided even the remotest semblance of inquiry after the physical well-being of his patient, though there was a certain yellowness about my host's eyes which argued a bilious habit of body." (p. 98) Less prominent people than Mr. Nosnibor, to be sure, may be avoided when they are ill of a crime, simply because the indisposition makes them less agreeable companions than those who are well. "The fact . . . that the Erewhonians attach none of that guilt to crime which they do to physical ailments, does not prevent the more selfish among them from neglecting a friend who has robbed a bank, for instance, till he has fully recovered; but it does prevent them from even thinking of treating criminals with that contemptuous tone which would seem to say, 'I, if I were you, should be a better man than you are,' a tone which is held quite reasonable in regard to physical ailment." (p. 92)

Since the treatment of the Erewhonian views of crime and disease pervades the whole book, Butler chooses by way of contrast a quite different method for his exposure of other aspects of Victorian life. The chapters on The Musical Banks, Ydgrun and the Ydgrunites, Birth Formulae, The Colleges of Unreason, and the Book of the Machines make separate little satiric allegories on the subjects of religion, convention, family life, education, and evolution in terms of machinery.

The mockery of Victorian religion gains much from the allegorical scheme under which Butler chooses to present it. The notion of religion as a second commercial system with banks "decorated in the most profuse fashion" and all the transactions "accompanied with music" (p. 137) sets ideas in motion at once about self-seeking in religious motive and sentimentality in religious practice. At the same time it provides an excellent frame for subsequent details such as the maintaining a balance in these banks by the respectable, though "the amount so kept had no direct commercial value in the outside world," the ladies' going alone, "except on state occasions" and carrying their purses "not exactly ostentatiously, yet just so as that those who met them should see whither they were going" (pp. 138–9), and the effort to bring the people back to the banks by putting fresh stained-glass windows in them and having the presidents

ride in omnibuses and talk nicely to the people and remember the ages of
the children and give them things when they are naughty. But there is
one lapse in the allegory. In expressing his view of the clergy Butler
almost forgets that they are supposed to be banking officials: "I sat opposite them and scanned their faces attentively. They did not please me;
they lacked, with few exceptions, the true Erewhonian frankness; and an
equal number from any other class would have looked happier and better
men. When I met them in the streets they did not seem like other people,
but had, as a general rule, a cramped expression upon their faces which
pained and depressed me. . . . I was always sorry for them, for in nine
cases out of ten they were well-meaning persons; they were in the main
very poorly paid; their constitutions were as a rule above suspicion; and
there were recorded numberless instances of their self-sacrifice and gen-
erosity; but they had had the misfortune to have been betrayed into a false
position at an age for the most part when their judgment was not ma-
tured, and after having been kept in studied ignorance of the real
difficulties of the system. But this did not make their position the less
a false one, and its bad effects upon themselves were unmistakable."
(pp. 147–8) Such sentences bear a striking resemblance to the passages
of comment on Butler's father in *The Way of All Flesh* and are no more
allegorical.

The order of ideas demands that this chapter should be followed, after
an interlude about Arowhena, by one on Ydgrun and the Ydgrunites,
for the true popular worship of Butler's day was that of Mrs. Grundy.
Higgs's attitude toward the deity is equivocal. He acknowledges that she
could be both cruel and absurd; yet he says: "Take her for all in all, however, she was a beneficent and useful deity, who did not care how much
she was denied so long as she was obeyed and feared, and who kept
hundreds of thousands in those paths which make life tolerably happy,
who would never have been kept there otherwise, and over whom a higher
and more spiritual ideal would have had no power." (p. 165) Butler is
speaking with undisguised admiration when he describes the "high
Ydgrunites" as "gentlemen in the full sense of the word." (p. 166) In the
original edition, he says of them that they were like "Englishmen who
had been educated at such schools as Winchester (if there be such another) and sent thence to one of the best colleges at Oxford or Cambridge." [9] In this chapter, Butler is writing largely under the spell of the
Victorian ideal which he is also partly mocking. The relative weakness of
the treatment may strike modern readers particularly because of the shift
in the demands of public opinion in the last seventy-five years; but its
basis lies in the absence of allegory. The analysis, with such satire as
there is, is given directly so that the pleasure of making the translation
from Erewhonian terms is lost. The deficiency is especially glaring since

9. *Erewhon or Over the Range* (London, 1872), p. 145.

the chapter comes after the one on Musical Banks, where the Erewhonian institution has a full being of its own and is not just made identical with the Church of England, which it portrays.

In the chapters on Birth Formulae and What They Mean by It, Butler's sense of irony reasserts itself. The allegorical conception here is deceptively simple. Butler merely makes explicit what he takes to be the assumption on which the Victorian family is based: that the parents have done the children a favor to let them come into the world and thus imposed a permanent obligation, one which is increased by their keeping the children dependent on them for money. These ideas are enough to "show the utter perversion of the Erewhonian mind." (p. 199) In the chapter called the World of the Unborn, which intervenes between the two on the family, Butler extends the satire by presenting the idea that leaving the world of the unborn is a sort of death for the soul. "The conditions which they must accept are so uncertain, that none but the most foolish of the unborn will consent to them; and it is from these, and these only, that our own ranks are recruited." (p. 183) Though the whole chapter shows Butler's keen interest in evolution and genetics and parallels some of the ideas set forth in *Life and Habit,* it does so without departing from the imaginative terms laid down in the conception itself.

In natural sequence after the chapters on the family come those on the Colleges of Unreason. Since Butler's views on the church and the family grow directly out of his own experience, it is rather startling to have him write with utter scorn of university education in spite of his own comparatively happy experience at Cambridge; but he is unsparing in his denunciation of the meaninglessness of classical studies.

> I met one youth who told me that for fourteen years the hypothetical language had been almost the only thing that he had been taught, although he had never (to his credit, as it seemed to me) shown the slightest proclivity towards it, while he had been endowed with not inconsiderable ability for several other branches of human learning. He assured me that he would never open another hypothetical book after he had taken his degree, but would follow out the bent of his own inclinations. This was well enough, but who could give him his fourteen years back again? (p. 214)

The hypothetical language is related to the study of hypothetics: "To imagine a set of utterly strange and impossible contingencies, and require the youths to give intelligent answers to the questions that arise therefrom, is reckoned the fittest conceivable way of preparing them for the actual conduct of their affairs in after life." (pp. 206–7) All this makes his point clearly enough through the allegory; but in his paragraphs of speculation about why the system does not do more harm to the natural good sense of the students, in which he finds the reasons in their not

paying "serious heed" to their training and in the "refining influence" of
the beauty of the surroundings, he has almost forgotten Erewhon and the
Colleges of Unreason to speak of English boys at the university. Again
the effectiveness of the satire flags as the allegory flags.

It is appropriately from a learned antiquary in the city of the colleges
that Higgs receives the Book of the Machines, which has brought about
the revolution of some five hundred years back when the Erewhonian
machines of more recent invention than two hundred and seventy-one
years before were destroyed. This book, which Higgs translates into
English, is Butler's often rewritten article, "Darwin among the Machines," from which the whole conception of Erewhon grew. The idea
which it presents, that the race of man is to be superseded by machines unless drastic measures are taken to prevent their development, seems in the
20th century to have been an ominous prophecy. Butler enforces the
gravity of the warning by letting the Erewhonians respond by destroying
all machines of recent origin, though not without a bloody revolution
and answers to the Book of the Machines, one of which is a rewriting of
another of Butler's early essays called "Lucubratio Ebris." The satiric
skill of the answer shows how cleverly Butler can mock both sides of a
question. He completely sustains his allegory in making the point that
machines are really extra members of man, simply grown outside the
body, and that man will always control them just as he now does his
extracorporeal members, "which are of more importance to him than a
good deal of his hair, or at any rate than his whiskers. His memory goes
into his pocket-book. He becomes more and more complex as he grows
older; he will then be seen with see-engines, or perhaps with artificial
teeth and hair: if he be a really well-developed specimen of his race, he
will be furnished with a large box upon wheels, two horses, and a coach-
man." (p. 258) The writer of the answer Butler makes allegorize the
worship of material power by classifying men according to horsepower.
In the revised edition the allegory is developed with a good deal of
luxuriance of detail: "Who shall deny that one who can tack on a special
train to his identity, and go wheresoever he will and whensoever he
pleases, is more highly organized than he who, should he wish for the
same power, might wish for the wings of a bird with an equal chance of
getting them; and whose legs are his only means of locomotion?" (pp.
258–9)

It is probably the chapters on the Book of the Machines which Butler
had especially in mind when he apologized for the lack of unity in *Erewhon*. They do make a longer and more detachable unit of treatment than
that accorded any other subject, and thus rather distort the proportions of
the book, though not nearly so much so in the original edition as in the
later one, where they are slightly expanded and have chapters on the
Rights of Animals and the Rights of Vegetables added on, so that the

interruption to the movement is twice as long as in the first edition. But
they are so rich in suggestiveness of thought and so full of the most animated play of Butler's imagination that they make one of the liveliest sections of the book. Nor are they really a digression from its method,
which has been discursive throughout. The ideas, to be sure, are presented
as coming from the work by an author long dead; but in being distinct and
entire in themselves, they are not different from the chapters on the
Musical Banks or any of the other subjects presented to judgment. In
sheer exuberance of mischief, they fit the spirit of the book; and like
other somersaults of Butler's mental acrobatics, they cannot be dismissed
as mere mischief. They share with other chapters of Higgs's stay in
Erewhon, the impression of comment on our own world made from a
point of view not quite upside down—or perhaps upside down and side-
wise as well—so that we see things never visible from the usual angle of
vision.

These chapters bring into special prominence the damage Butler did to
his book by revision. It is the additions which are detrimental; and Butler
made them unwillingly. He accounts for his tampering with his early
work:

> *I am still fairly well satisfied with those parts of "Erewhon" that were
> repeatedly rewritten, but from those that had only a single writing I
> would gladly cut out some forty or fifty pages if I could.*
>
> *This, however, may not be, for the copyright will probably expire
> in a little over twelve years. It was necessary, therefore, to revise the
> book throughout for literary inelegancies—of which I found many
> more than I had expected—and also to make such substantial additions
> as should secure a new lease of life—at any rate for the copyright. If,
> then, instead of cutting out, say fifty pages, I have been compelled to
> add about sixty invitâ Minervâ—the blame rests neither with my pub-
> lisher nor with me, but with the copyright laws. Nevertheless I can
> assure the reader that, though I have found it an irksome task to take
> up work which I thought I had got rid of thirty years ago, and much of
> which I am ashamed of, I have done my best to make the new matter
> savor so much of the better portions of the old, that none but the best
> critics shall perceive at what places the gaps of between thirty and
> forty years occur.* (pp. xiv–v)

The revisions of style are for the most part indifferent, though it is a
help in ease of reading to have the immensely long paragraphs of the
original broken up.[1] The season of the year and the direction of the journey to the metropolis are changed, but without any noticeable change in
effect. The excisions, though slight, are nearly always improvements.

1. I have not seen the second edition, but I assume from Butler's preface to it that
even this change did not come until the revision of 1901.

They remove superfluous comments at the ends of chapters, such as: "With these thoughts I started on my downward journey," at the end of chapter vi; and "I also propose to give certain other Erewhonian views of things in general, which I shall never arrive at if I do not hurry on a little faster," at the end of chapter ix. They take out some of the insistent references to Italy and one rather long explanation of the value of clarity in painting. The Handelian arias with which Higgs brings tears to Yram's eyes are changed to English ballads, and the comparison with Giorgione is left out of the description of the Erewhonian type of beauty. Altogether the impression is that Butler was a sound critic of the earlier work in pruning it.

But nearly all the major additions one wishes away. They are consistently detrimental to the allegorical, and hence to the satiric, effect. They begin in the chapter called Current Opinions, where it certainly would not take one of Butler's "best critics" to feel the awkwardness of the comparison of Erewhonian views with those of the Mohammedans, the Maories, and the Italians, which intrudes upon the introduction of the Erewhonian mind as something distinct in itself and related to ours only by its allegorical significance. The explanation of the euphemism of stealing socks for being indisposed is forced; and the paragraphs which end the chapter by explaining that the straighteners train themselves by experiencing all the moral defects they must learn to cure confuse the point about English medicine and morality. The idea of any sort of misfortune as culpable is perhaps the chief revision in thought and is thrust in at various places, doing the greatest artistic damage in the chapter on Erewhonian trials. The addition of the accounts of the trials of other unfortunates dissipates the tremendous allegorical and satiric impact of the original trial of the consumptive. At the end of the chapter on Musical Banks, Butler puts in a preparation for *Erewhon Revisited,* which was now of course already written, by saying that the country was ripe for a change of religion; and a few paragraphs earlier he breaks the allegory by directly pointing the comparison with England. In the chapter on the Colleges of Unreason, he adds a rather tedious section on the professors' fear of giving themselves away, which has little to do with what he has been discussing. The only additions which contribute more than the length which the copyright demanded are those in the Book of the Machines. The chief revision here is the example of the spade as an extension of a man's arm, which fits the point to be made and the feeling of the essay, as does the enlargement of the discussion of classifying men by horsepower.

By far the most extended and the most unfortunate additions are the two chapters which follow as a sort of appendage to the Book of the Machines revealing other strange notions of the Erewhonians. The Rights of Animals and The Rights of Vegetables give some amusing comment on the stratagems of rationalization to which common sense is reduced in evading fanatical views. For instance, the judge finds that animals, whom it is unlawful to kill, may be killed in self-defense. "Hardly had this decision become known before a number of animals hitherto harmless, took to attacking their owners with such ferocity, that it became necessary to put them to a natural death." (p. 267) This is funny enough, but it adds nothing to the conception of the Erewhonians or ourselves; and it grows tedious when it is spun out in another chapter giving the evasions of the protective laws for vegetables. These two chapters, the only ones wholly new in the revised edition, lack the spontaneity which is the distinctive quality of the rest of the book; and their position just before Butler leaves the presentation of ideas for the return to physical action in the chapter on the Escape gives them a deplorable prominence. The reader must agree with Butler in being sad that the copyright laws compelled him to pad the fresh work of his youth with these rather jaded additions that weaken the allegory.

But it would be ungracious to leave on a note of complaint a work which, in spite of the compulsory reworking, retains vitality as its characteristic mark. Butler succeeds even in the revised book in making a vigorous comment on the realm of Victorian ideas through the vividly realized allegorical realm of Erewhon.

7

Future Worlds

"Mundus alter et idem"
BISHOP JOSEPH HALL

IT IS rather a comment on the temper of the times than on the methods of satiric allegory that the worlds of the future used to judge present conditions take such different forms in the 19th and the 20th centuries. For the Victorians, the dreams of the future were characteristically visions which showed up the defects of the real world by revealing the "peace and rest, and cleanness and smiling goodwill" [1] of a society without flaws. For our generation, hagridden by perpetual war and totalitarianism, the dreams of the future are nightmares in which the evils of our day have reached their ultimate conclusion of the destruction of the nature of man. The fundamental difference in attitude and emotional impetus behind the writing makes the works of the two periods entirely different in technique and in the effects produced.

Two characteristic 19th-century dreams of the future, *News from Nowhere* and *Looking Backward,* are projected as actual dreams, the first taking place in normal sleep after an evening of discussion of "the future of the fully-developed new society" (p. 3) and the other happening in a sleep produced by hypnosis after a day of personal emotion in which the hero is troubled by conditions of the times only as the current strikes, which "had been nearly incessant ever since the great business crisis of 1873," [2] delay the completion of the house he is building in preparation for his marriage. The ideal worlds of which the two narrators dream are somewhat different; but the panacea which has cured the old evils of the world in both is socialism, or as Morris repeatedly calls it, *pure* communism.

Morris's world of the future is shaped by a nostalgia for the past. It is an idyl of the earthly paradise colored by the soft glow of medieval stained glass. The air is fragrant with delicious perfumes of flowers and old herb

1. William Morris, *News from Nowhere, Collected Works of William Morris,* ed. May Morris (London, 1912), *16,* 4. All quotations are from this edition.
2. Edward Bellamy, *Looking Backward, 2000–1887* (Boston, 1890), p. 15. All quotations are from this edition.

gardens. The people are endowed with health and almost perpetual youth so that the hero guesses the age of a woman of forty-two to be twenty, while he, bearing the traces of the life he has lived in the real world, at "hard on fifty-six" seems to them immensely aged. What strikes him most forcibly is their happy friendliness; and he at once adopts their habit of addressing each other as "neighbour."

The primary condition of such happiness, as might be expected in a world created by Morris to show the defects of his own, is beauty in surroundings and in all objects of use, which are the products of happy craftsmen. His picture of Hammersmith is characteristic:

> King Street was gone, and the highway ran through wide sunny meadows and garden-like tillage. The Creek, which we crossed at once, had been rescued from its culvert, and as we went over its pretty bridge we saw its waters, yet swollen by the tide, covered with gay boats of different sizes. There were houses about, some on the road, some amongst the fields with pleasant lanes leading down to them, and each surrounded by a teeming garden. They were all pretty in design, and as solid as might be, but countryfied in appearance, like yeomen's dwellings; some of them of red brick like those by the river, but more of timber and plaster, which were by the necessity of their construction so like medieval houses of the same materials that I fairly felt as if I were alive in the fourteenth century; a sensation helped out by the costume of the people that we met or passed, in whose dress there was nothing "modern." Almost everybody was gaily dressed, but especially the women, who were so well-looking, or even so handsome, that I could scarcely refrain my tongue from calling my companion's attention to the fact. Some faces I saw that were thoughtful, and in these I noticed great nobility of expression, but none that had a glimmer of unhappiness, and the greater part (we came upon a good many people) were frankly and openly joyous. (p. 23)

The sense of the past is also suggested by the architecture of the public buildings, which combines the best qualities of "the Gothic of northern Europe with those of the Saracenic and Byzantine, though there was no copying of any one of these styles." (p. 24) Morris uses numerous symbols of the relation between beauty in a product and joy in making it. Every object from the tall glasses used in the communal eating halls, where the meals are appropriately delicious, to the pipe given the hero at the tobacconist's shop, is a delight to the eye and has been made with pleasure in its craftsmanship. The hero, for whom Morris rather fittingly supplies only the generic name of Guest, never tires of describing the beauty of the clothing, which is graceful in line and charming in color and in the texture of silk or linen or wool. Since there is no dirty work, there is no reason for dark or ugly clothes, though a reader from our world cannot help wondering about the after-work state of the costumes of the haymakers: "young women clad . . . not mostly in silk, but in light woollen most gaily embroidered; the men being all clad in white flannel embroidered in bright colours. The meadow looked like a gigantic tulip-bed because of them. All hands were working deliberately but well and steadily, though they were as noisy with merry talk as a grove of autumn starlings." (p. 154)

Joy in work is insisted upon as much as is the general beauty. Such shape as the narrative has is created by the pastoral journey up the Thames to participate in the pleasure of harvesting. The only people who will not take part in the general festival of haymaking are a group called the "obstinate refusers" who are so entranced with the "easy-hard" work they are doing in making the decorative carving on a new building (created, like many of the buildings in this world of the future, to replace a 19th-century monstrosity) that they do not want to stop even to go into the fields. The chapter about them was added for the first English edition after the version which came out serially in *Commonweal* and the American edition of 1890. Morris apparently felt that he needed to insist further upon the joy of work which creates beauty. In keeping with his judgment on the industrial system, Morris has banished factories from his allegorical vision, though there are "Banded-workshops" to do "handwork in which working together is necessary or convenient." (p. 46) He allows furnaces, though of course without smoke, for making glass and pottery, and makes power available wherever the people live for whatever purposes it can best fulfill. The view of property is demonstrated in the episode at the tobacconist's, which shows Guest that shops exist only to give out what people want. He is served by a solicitous child, as eager to be helpful as is the maiden who holds the horse in the street so that Guest and his guide may go into the shop.

The long exposition of the new order given ostensibly to Guest by a benevolent antiquarian, versed enough in the old ways to make the new ones intelligible, is all too clearly for the reader's benefit. The comment on the real world is almost explicit in the details: with the abolition of property, government as well as business has practically disappeared from this world of happy communists; so has the whole idea of punishment and most crime (such crimes of passion as do still occur are followed by repentance and atonement); divorce courts have gone, since "all the cases that came into them were matters of property quarrels" (p. 56), and couples may separate and come together again upon consent. Indeed, Dick and Clara, the happy couple who are Guest's hosts, are in the act of such a reconciliation while the old man is expounding the society. Education, like everything else, exemplifies the creed of joy: children learn what they have a desire to learn, and bookishness is not encouraged. Dick has an actual dislike of it, though he says: "You see, children are mostly given to imitating their elders, and when they see most people about them engaged in genuinely amusing work, like house-building and street-paving, and gardening, and the like, that is what they want to be doing; so I don't think we need fear having too many book-learned men." (p. 31) The antiquarian, to be sure, is a lover of books; but he is wholly committed to the new mode of education. His view of what passed for it in early times is utterly contemptuous: "But of course I understand," he says to Guest—and to Morris's audience—

> your point of view about education, which is that of times past, when "the struggle for life," as men used to phrase it (i.e., the struggle for a slave's rations on one side, and for a bouncing share of the slave-holders' privilege on the other), pinched "education" for most people into a niggardly dole of not very accurate information; something to be swallowed by the beginner in the art of living whether he liked it or not, and was hungry for it or not: and which had been chewed and digested over and over again by people who didn't care about it in order to serve it out to other people who didn't care about it. (p. 63)

The real clue to the joyous society in which everyone does what he likes and likes to do right is given by the old man when he says: "When we are children time passes so slow with us that we seem to have time for everything. . . . At least let us rejoice that we have got back our childhood again. I drink to the days that are." (p. 102) Morris calls his book "some chapters in a utopian romance"; and his particular utopia has the quality of a never-never land where perpetual childhood prevails. The mirror he holds up to his own society shows clearly enough the defects he deplores; but Victorian England, with all its faults, seems preferable to the unending holiday of his imagined world. There is a cloying sweetness in his earthly paradise that makes the reader wish, like Clara, for some of the excitement of the novels of real life, even though they depict the evil nature of man. "How is it," she asks, "that we find the dreadful times of the past so interesting to us—in pictures and poetry?" (p. 102) In her question Morris suggests the inadequacy of his utopia. What is finally disgusting in the transformation he works on the world is not its unreality, but its uninterestingness. We grow bored with this world of good children and with Morris's management of the whole allegory as if it were a moral bedtime story for children instead of a serious criticism of society.

The people of Bellamy's vision of the future inhabit a more adult and more interesting world. His inadequacy is a specifically artistic one. Like Morris, he starts from a formula for the regeneration of society; but his reorganization of the existing order is highly complex. Since Morris's formula seems to be a return to pastoral simplicity, there is no disharmony between the idea and the rather dull pastoral which results from it. Bellamy has tried more strenuously to cope with actual problems of production and distribution, and he earnestly wishes to make his solutions clear. But at the same time, he too wishes to write a romance, or at least to coat the pill of didacticism. He gives himself away in the preface: "Warned by a teacher's experience that learning is accounted a weariness to the flesh, the author has sought to alleviate the instructive quality of the book by casting it in the form of a romantic narrative, which he would be glad to fancy not wholly devoid of interest on its own account." (p. iv) The story is avowedly just for the purpose of making palatable Dr. Leete's explanations of social institutions. It is true that Bellamy arouses a fair degree of interest in the narrative of Julian West (his hero fortunately has a proper name) and Edith Leete, who turns out to be the great granddaughter of the girl to whom Julian had been engaged before he fell asleep; but the core of the book is in the long disquisitions of Edith's father about the organization of society, which regularly take place after the ladies have retired, "leaving Dr. Leete and myself alone." (p. 47) These too are interesting, and rather more successful as essays than the love story is as narrative; but Bellamy leaves them to return to the story as abruptly as he left the story to start them so that he constantly reminds the reader of his confession in the preface that he is just decorating his body of idea with a tale as a teacher's ruse. The judgment is delivered in a treatise rather than in the constructed allegory. Since the thought is not digested into the imaginative framework, the book falls to pieces as a work of art.

When Julian is allowed to learn from Edith, the love story and the instruction about the new era are necessarily combined. As he goes shopping with her in one of the magnificent public buildings, he learns that the ward stores contain samples of all the goods in the central warehouse, that orders are sent by pneumatic tube and so quickly filled that what they have purchased will probably be delivered before they reach home, and that payment is made by punching the appropriate amount from a credit card instead of being simply waived as in Morris's utopia. In the same way, it is from Edith's offering him music that he first learns the magic of sounds brought to the homes by the mere pressing of a button, from the central halls where they are produced. Julian's learning from Edith provides Bellamy with a good chance to underline his point by contrasting the Boston of the year 2000 with that of the year 1887, for she is more ignorant than her father is of old times and asks Julian about them in dismay. Her distress at the idea of salespeople who tried to persuade a customer to buy and at the plight of music lovers who had to go to concerts to hear fine music increases Julian's sense of the inferiority of the bad old times; and all the while Edith herself is making the new ones more attractive to him.

But in most of the scenes between them, she is simply comforting him for the strange experience he is passing through, and he is simply adoring her beauty and kindness. The love affair, from his waking to the sound of her whispered "Promise me, then, that you will not tell him" (p. 27), through his seizing her hand in order to hold on to his sense of identity after his unnerving solitary walk through the strange new Boston and the various scenes of her solicitude about his welfare, until she declares her love for him in the underground room which is all that is left of his old life: all this could take place without any reference to satire or to allegory. It is a story which exists in its own right and is quite distinct from the ideological part of the work.

Conversely, Dr. Leete's analyses of conditions are distinct entities and depend in no way on the fact that his hearer is in love with his daughter, whose existence both interlocutors seem to forget throughout the long conversations. It is from Dr. Leete that Julian learns about the organization of society as a huge industrial army, a monopoly which has literally ended all monopolies. Since the credit card pay of all workers is equal, the incentive for advancement, as in military life, is solely honor. The reorganization of society on the principle of cooperation has made actual armies unnecessary; federal union has been achieved, and the expectation is that the world will become one nation. But Bellamy glorifies army discipline. In the nightmare in which Julian thinks he has returned to the old Boston, he sees a military parade: "It was the first sight in that dreary day which had inspired me with any other emotions than wondering pity and amazement. Here at last were order and reason, an exhibition of what intelligent coöperation can accomplish." (p. 322) It is easy to see that such a sentence as the following was written while glamor still attached to military life: "By requiring of every man his best you have made God his task-master, and by making honor the sole reward of achievement you have imparted to all service the distinction peculiar in my day to the soldier's." (p. 159 n.) The general-in-chief of the new great army is the President of the United States; and government is largely the management of industrial affairs. Dr. Leete's lecture has to go on in many installments, however, for besides industry and government it covers education, now compulsory for "half a dozen higher grades" (p. 217) than in the earlier Massachusetts, and providing for professional training for those who are suited to it; the care of the ill and disabled and those who are atavistic enough to have committed crimes; and especially the expounding of the idea of the brotherhood of man—as a conviction and not a form of words—on which the whole society rests.

In one episode involving the whole family Julian is allowed to learn as he does from Edith by participating in action instead of listening to her father talk. The family's taking him out to dine gives an opportunity for explaining the system of public kitchens from which the food can be sent to private homes, as it has been to the Leetes' for the first few days of

Julian's visit, or enjoyed in the community dining halls. There are lessons to be learned on the way to the hall. A heavy rainstorm during the day has convinced the visitor from the 19th century that the condition of the streets will make it impossible to leave the house; yet the ladies appear at the dinner hour "prepared to go out, but without either rubbers or umbrellas." He finds the mystery explained by a "continuous waterproof covering . . . let down so as to enclose the sidewalk and turn it into a well lighted and perfectly dry corridor, which was filled with a stream of ladies and gentlemen dressed for dinner." (p. 151) As usual, Julian has a chance to explain to the amazed Edith the necessity for boots and umbrellas in the Boston of an earlier day; and Dr. Leete, true to his role of mentor, "overhearing something of our talk, turned to say that the difference between the age of individualism and that of concert was well characterized by the fact that, in the nineteenth century, when it rained, the people of Boston put up three hundred thousand umbrellas over as many heads, and in the twentieth century they put up one umbrella over all the heads." (p. 152) It is perhaps a slip natural to the system on which the book is constructed that Edith, who has not heard of umbrellas when the walk started, then remarks: "The private umbrella is father's favorite figure to illustrate the old way when everybody lived for himself and his family. There is a nineteenth century painting at the Art Gallery representing a crowd of people in the rain, each one holding his umbrella over himself and his wife, and giving his neighbors the drippings, which he claims must have been meant by the artist as a satire on his times." (p. 152) The hall, where they have an excellent meal served in their own dining room, Dr. Leete uses to point out another advantage of the new society, for it is "in fact, a part of our house, slightly detached from the rest." (p. 153) Julian's enlightenment about the classless society comes when dinner is perfectly served by a youth who has none of the servility of the old servant class and who is undoubtedly highly educated and the social equal of the people he is serving. In the course of explaining to Edith the meaning of the obsolete word "menial" it is casually mentioned that Dr. Leete was a waiter himself in this very dining hall forty years before.

His being now retired and at what is generally considered the best part of life affords the opportunity to explain the view of age. One way in which the whole book seems more mature than *News from Nowhere* is that while there is great concern for the health and education of the young people, there is no worship of youth. The time from twenty to forty is spent in the service of the state; and after that "the higher and larger activities . . . that are considered the main business of existence" can be entered upon. People regard later life as "a time for the leisurely and unperturbed appreciation of the good things of the world which they have helped to create." (p. 196) They are equipped to enjoy this leisure be-

cause they are intelligent human beings who enjoy using their minds and
have cultivated them from youth up. The general interest in things of the
mind has created "an era of unexampled intellectual splendor. . . .
[Upon] the rise of the race to a new plane of existence with an illimitable
vista of progress, their minds were affected in all their faculties with a
stimulus, of which the outburst of the mediaeval renaissance offers a suggestion but faint indeed." (p. 161) Julian apparently finds this claim of
Dr. Leete borne out by the fineness of the novels of Berrian, about which
he is understandably vague. Needless to say, the reader never quite be-
lieves in the new renaissance.

Altogether, Bellamy succeeds in convincing the mind that the world
he talks about would be an interesting one in which to live; but he never
succeeds in giving it imaginative existence. He wishes to persuade the
feelings; but he does so only when he approaches them through intellectual analysis, to which the story is extraneous. The inspiration of his
work is allegorical, as he proclaims in the little introductory allegory of
the society of his day: rich people as passengers riding in a coach pulled
by the poor. But he does not know how to sustain an allegory. He escapes
the intolerable sentimentality of Morris; but he lacks even Morris's degree of indirection in his comment on the world he condemns. Consequently, though the satire of 19th-century society is clear, he never makes
his allegorical vehicle carry it. *Looking Backward* is so unsatisfying a
work of allegorical art that it is unsatisfying also as satire.

The characteristic future world created by satirists of our own day is
made not by contrast with the world that exists but by an enlarged likeness of it. The vehicle of their satire is simply an extension of the present.
Their mood is indicated by the quotation from Berdiaeff which Aldous
Huxley uses as the epigraph for *Brave New World:*

> *Les utopies apparaissent comme bien plus réalisable qu'on ne le croyait
> autrefois. Et nous nous trouvons actuellement devant une question bien
> autrement angoissante: Comment éviter leur réalisation définitive?
> . . . Les utopies sont réalisables. La vie marche vers les utopies. Et
> peut-être un siècle nouveau commence-t-il, un siècle où les intellectuels
> et la classe cultivée rêveront aux moyens d'éviter les utopies et de
> retourner à une société non utopique, moins "parfaite" et plus libre.*[3]

What gives the special nightmare quality to these utopias that the writers
fear is that they do seem all too realizable. They have the dreadful
actuality of a dream which is not dissipated by any waking. The authenticity of the horror is thus the double one of grotesque distortion of an hal-
lucination which we long to escape and of the truth which we can test with

3. All quotations are from the edition of New York, 1946.

our faculties awake. They are convincing to the imagination because they are the logical development of phenomena which we are compelled to observe every day. Two of the most overpowering of them are Huxley's *Brave New World* and Orwell's *Nineteen Eighty-four*. The inhabitants of Huxley's world, where "Civilization is sterilization," and "Cleanliness is next to Fordliness," are nearly all happy. Those in Orwell's live in filth and discomfort and are mostly miserable; but to the reader, compelled in each case by the spell of the imagination to live to the end of the book and after in these worlds of the future, the happiness and the unhappiness are equally horrible, for the conclusion of both is that no one can "end as a man."

Part of the convincingness in both comes from the fact that the authors have been willing to dispense with the dreamer from our day who is transported into the new world. The dreamer is perforce the reader; and there is no lecturing him under the thin disguise of explaining the scheme of life to a newcomer in it. The exposition is, nevertheless, there; and it is managed with consummate skill by both authors. The initiation into Huxley's world of the future comes through a tour from the Fertilizing Room to a nursery where sleeping children are having by hypnopaedia their lesson in Elementary Class Consciousness. The symbol of its reduction to a system is the whisper under every pillow of the Beta children:

> all wear green, . . . and Delta Children wear khaki. Oh no, I don't want to play with Delta children. And Epsilons are still worse. They're too stupid to be able to read or write. Besides they wear black, which is such a beastly colour. I'm *so* glad I'm a Beta. . . . Alpha children wear grey. They work much harder than we do, because they're so frightfully clever. I'm really awfully glad I'm a Beta, because I don't work so hard. And then we are much better than the Gammas and Deltas. Gammas are stupid. They all wear green, and Delta children wear khaki. (pp. 30–1)

and so on in an endless round of "Suggestions from the State" until the eloquence of the Director of Hatcheries and Conditioning, who is conducting the tour of students leads him to bang the table. " 'Oh, Ford!' he said in another tone, 'I've gone and woken the children.' " (p. 32) Already the symbols of dehumanized man have been set forth as the students learn on the tour about how babies are hatched from bottles in incubators in "this year of stability, A. F. 632" (p. 3), with Alphas and Betas bottled separately, "one egg, one embryo, one adult" (p. 5) and the Gammas, Deltas, and Epsilons indefinitely multiplied by Bokanovsky's Process into endless numbers of identical twins suited by their lack of mentality and stunted growth to perform contentedly the tasks for which "Even Epsilons are useful," because the babies are not merely hatched: "We also predestinate and condition. We decant our babies as socialized hu-

man beings, as Alphas or Epsilons, as future sewage workers or future
. . . Directors of Hatcheries." (p. 14) At the same time, the tour also
serves as a scathing satire on modern education. As the students follow
the Director and Henry Foster, the statistician, busily trying to get the
right words of wisdom into their little black notebooks, their response is
as automatic as that of the embryos on the conveyor belts to the injections
that "immunize the fish against the future man's diseases." (p. 18) " 'I
shall begin at the beginning,' said the D.H.C. and the more zealous students recorded his intention in their notebooks: *Begin at the beginning."
(p. 3) He defines bokanovskification as " 'a series of arrests of development. We check the normal growth and, paradoxically enough, the egg
responds by budding.' *Responds by budding.* The pencils were busy."
(p. 5) When Mr. Foster points upward to the racks of bottles, "like
chickens drinking, the students lifted their eyes towards the distant ceil-
ing." (p. 11) By the time we have gone with the "desperately scrib-
bling" students through the garden and watched the children at the erotic
play which begins their immunization against true passion, we have been
inescapably drawn into this appalling world of "Community, Identity,
Stability." (p. 6)

In his third chapter, by skillful management of the stream of consciousness technique, Huxley assails his readers with the responses to their
world from half a dozen of its denizens at once. There is first his ford-
ship Mustapha Mond, the Resident Controller of Western Europe, continuing the indoctrination of the students by expounding to them the
"inspired saying of Our Ford's: History is bunk" (p. 38) and the folly
of the old times when there was the squalor of homes, "a few small
rooms, stiflingly overinhabited by a man, by a periodically teeming
woman, by a rabble of boys and girls of all ages. No air, no space; an
understerilized prison; darkness, disease, and smells" (pp. 41–2); the
obscenity of fathers and mothers, husbands, wives, lovers, monogamy,
and romance. "Our Ford—or Our Freud, as, for some inscrutable reason,
he chose to call himself whenever he spoke of psychological matters—
our Freud had been the first to reveal the appalling dangers of family
life. The world was full of fathers—was therefore full of misery; full of
mothers—therefore of every kind of perversion from sadism to chastity,
full of brothers, sisters, uncles, aunts—full of madness and suicide."
(p. 44) Second, there is the sensible young girl Fanny Crowne, who is
about to take a pregnancy substitute since she has been feeling rather out
of sorts lately; and we hear interspersed with the Controller's remarks
her conversation in the GIRL'S DRESSING ROOM, where "Torrents
of hot water were splashing into or gurgling out of a hundred baths.
Rumbling and hissing, eighty vibro-vacuum massage machines were
simultaneously kneading and sucking the firm and sunburnt flesh of
eighty superb female specimens. Every one was talking at the top of her

voice. A Synthetic Music machine was warbling out a super-cornet solo." (p. 41) Fanny is trying to bring Lenina Crowne, probably not her near kinswoman since "the two thousand million inhabitants of the planet had only ten thousand names between them" (p. 41) to some sense of the impropriety of having gone steadily with Henry Foster for four months, and especially without having another man during all this time. She preaches the convention of promiscuity in a coaxing tone; and when Lenina, whom we have already seen in the Conditioning Room making a date with Henry Foster, confesses that she has not been "feeling very keen on promiscuity lately," Fanny nods in sympathy and understanding and answers, "But one's got to make the effort, . . . one's got to play the game. After all, every one belongs to every one else." (p. 50) A third theme in this contrapuntal chapter is the response of Bernard Marx, who turns pale as he overhears Henry Foster: " 'Lenina Crowne?' said Henry Foster, echoing the Assistant Predestinator's question as he zipped up his trousers. 'Oh, she's a splendid girl. Wonderfully pneumatic. I'm surprised you haven't had her.' " (p. 51) Bernard's intelligence is Alpha plus; but he is so small of stature that the gossip has it that alcohol got into his blood-surrogate by mistake while he was still in the bottle. Consequently, he has stirrings of being an individual; and to Lenina, whom he objects to hearing discussed as if she were meat, he seems so queer that only Fanny's prodding and the first stirrings of boredom with Henry Foster can make her encourage his advances. He is a specialist on hypnopaedia; so when he hears the platitudes which others utter as axioms, he thinks to himself, "One hundred repetitions three nights a week for four years, . . . Sixty-two thousand four hundred repetitions make one truth. Idiots!" (p. 55) The bits that we are given from these sources of consciousness grow shorter and shorter as the chapter goes on so that we are whirled round and round from one to the other in a sort of vertiginous horror.

By the time Bernard and Lenina meet in the lift, we are thoroughly aware of their temperaments and of the use Huxley intends to make of their contrasting points of view. We are prepared for Lenina's friendly way of hailing Bernard to cry that she would love to come to New Mexico with him for a week in July and thus to make a public announcement that she is returning to decorum and being unfaithful to Henry. Huxley emphasizes their natures by their responses when the Epsilon-Minus Semi-Moron elevator operator lets them out on the roof to take planes to go to their various engagements. When Bernard looks at the sky and says, "Isn't it beautiful!" she smiles at him "with an expression of the most sympathetic understanding," and says, "Simply perfect for Obstacle Golf." (p. 71) Huxley's images make vivid Bernard's state of mind. His wretchedness, after the magnificently normal Benito Hoover has tried to cheer him up with a gramme of *soma,* is like that of "a man pursued,

but pursued by enemies he does not wish to see, lest they should seem
more hostile even than he had supposed, and he himself be made to feel
guiltier and even more helplessly alone." (p. 75) He thinks back upon his
dreaming of the rapture of having the popular Lenina say yes to his
proposal to come to New Mexico:

> Well, now she had said it and he was still wretched—wretched that
> she should have thought it such a perfect afternoon for Obstacle Golf,
> that she should have trotted away to join Henry Foster, that she should
> have found him funny for not wanting to talk of their most private
> affairs in public. Wretched, in a word, because she had behaved as any
> healthy and virtuous English girl ought to behave and not in some
> other, abnormal extraordinary way.

He is self-conscious enough to declare to himself, "I am I, and I wish I
wasn't." (pp. 75–6) It is through these two points of view that life in the
Fordian era is principally revealed, both in its outward aspects and in the
effects of its conditioning on two temperaments which it has damaged
in opposite ways.

Lenina always has the proper reactions. She epitomizes the *erzatz*
quality of this world in which *surrogate* seems to be the key word, for not
only are the embryos nourished on blood-surrogate, but after they are
decanted, they move through a world of champagne-surrogate, and oboe-
surrogate music, with buildings of carrara-surrogate, and belts of
morocco-surrogate such as Lenina, who gives much attention to clothes,
wears with pride. Huxley deftly uses her conversation, of which they
make the inevitable staple, to convey many of the slogans of the sleep
teaching, by which Alphas and Betas, who still do have minds, are supposed to live. A good example is the exchange which takes place in the
ice cream *soma* bar between her and the sulking Bernard, whom she has
coaxed away from an afternoon walk on Skiddaw to the Semi-Demi-
Finals of the Women's Heavyweight Wrestling Championship in Amsterdam, where he has been cross to all her friends "and in spite of his
misery absolutely refused to take the half-gramme raspberry sundae which
she pressed upon him."

> "I'd rather be myself," he said. "Myself and nasty. Not somebody
> else, however jolly."
> "A gramme in time saves nine," said Lenina, producing a bright
> treasure of sleep-taught wisdom.
> Bernard pushed away the proffered glass impatiently.
> "Now don't lose your temper," she said. "Remember, one cubic
> centimetre cures ten gloomy sentiments."
> "Oh, for Ford's sake, be quiet!" he shouted.
> Lenina shrugged her shoulders. "A gramme is always better than

a damn," she concluded with dignity, and drank the sundae herself.
(p. 105)

Whenever slogans fail Lenina, she has recourse to *soma.* The episode in
Amsterdam shows how closely linked in allegorical function are the
slogans and *soma,* both of which at once symbolize the dehumanized state
of man and help to cause it. The Controller has already explained the
uses of *soma:*

> Now—such is progress—the old men work, the old men copulate, the
> old men have no time, no leisure from pleasure, not a moment to sit
> down and think—or if ever by some unlucky chance such a crevice of
> time should yawn in the solid substance of their distractions, there
> is always *soma,* delicious *soma,* half a gramme for a half-holiday, a
> gramme for a week-end, two grammes for a trip to the gorgeous East,
> three for a dark eternity on the moon; returning whence they find
> themselves on the other side of the crevice, safe on the solid ground of
> daily labour and distraction, scampering from feely to feely, from girl
> the pneumatic girl, from Electro-magnetic Golf course to . . . (pp.
> 66–7)

The reader is left wondering what lies beyond Golf for the old men. Huxley's interruptions of his speakers are often significant. But *soma* is useful
not only to old men. It is Lenina who is chiefly used to communicate its
powers. She keeps her bottle constantly ready and takes doses according
to the degree of holiday she needs. *Soma* is served with the coffee after
the excellent meal in the dining room of Henry Foster's apartment house;
and before they go off to dance at the Westminster Abbey Cabaret,
Lenina has taken her two half-gramme tablets and Henry his three.

> Five-stepping with the other four hundred round and round West-
> minster Abbey, Lenina and Henry were yet dancing in another world
> —the warm, the richly coloured, the infinitely friendly world of *soma*-
> holiday. How kind, how good-looking, how delightfully amusing every
> one was! . . . And when, exhausted, the Sixteen had laid by their
> sexophones and the Synthetic Music apparatus was producing the very
> latest in slow Malthusian Blues, they might have been twin embryos
> gently rocking together on the waves of a bottled ocean of blood-
> surrogate. (p. 91)

It is the fact that her *soma* bottle has been misplaced that makes the realities of the savage reservation in New Mexico almost unendurable to
Lenina, so that "As soon as they got back to the rest-house, she swallowed
six half-gramme tablets of *soma,* lay down on her bed, and within ten
minutes had embarked for lunar eternity. It would be eighteen hours at
the least before she was in time again." (p. 167) Huxley shows how when

the bottle is at hand, it helps her through all emergencies, small and great. Half a gramme will save her from boredom: "When the Warden started booming, she had inconspicuously swallowed half a gramme of *soma,* with the result that she could now sit, serenely not listening, thinking of nothing at all, but with her large blue eyes fixed on the Warden's face in an expression of rapt attention." (p. 119) Sometimes there is a slight difficulty in deciding just how much to anaesthetize herself. After the Savage has refused to make love to her, she faces this problem: "One gramme, she decided, would not be enough; hers had been more than a one-gramme affliction. But if she took two grammes, she ran the risk of not waking up in time to-morrow morning. She compromised and, into her cupped left palm, shook out three half-gramme tablets." (p. 204)

Bernard's point of view is contrasted with Lenina's in this as in other matters. He resists taking *soma* in moderation like a normal Fordian. He clings to the absurd notion that he would like to be himself, even though he does not like himself; and this involves staying conscious. But when he can bear himself and his companions no longer, he takes doses of four tablets at once. He steels himself in this fashion for his first night with Lenina, after she has succeeded in convincing him that she is incapable of any sort of love-making except what the erotic play of her childhood and the Malthusian drill of her schooldays have prepared her for. Again after the collapse of his brief career of shining in society in the reflected glow of the Savage he has brought back from the reservation, "Punctured, utterly deflated, he dropped into a chair and, covering his face with his hands, began to weep. A few minutes later, however, he thought better of it and took four tablets of *soma.*" (p. 210)

While Lenina reveals by assent the soporific powers of slogans, sex, and *soma.* Bernard gives by his resistance to them some of the fundamental conceptions on which the society is based. The keystone of the belief in our Ford, "Ford's in his flivver, all's well with the world," he scorns as he does the other catchwords. He goes through the mumbo-jumbo of the Solidarity Circle of the Ford's Day celebration undrugged by the delirium from the first Solidarity Hymn:

> *Ford, we are twelve; oh, make us one,*
> *   Like drops within the Social River;*
> *Oh, make us now together run*
> *   As swiftly as thy shining Flivver.* (p. 95)

through the last:

> *Orgy-porgy, Ford and fun,*
> *   Kiss the girls and make them One.*
> *Boys at one with girls at peace;*
> *   Orgy-porgy gives release.* (p. 100)

Huxley skillfully uses Bernard's isolation to accentuate the travesty of religious and emotional experience. Bernard remains alone even through the orgiastic communal embraces which end the ceremony, though he miserably lies, "Yes, I thought it was wonderful," when Fifi Bradlaugh looks at him rapturously and says, "Wasn't it wonderful? Wasn't it simply wonderful?" (p. 100)

It is Bernard who puts into words the belief in infantilism which Lenina simply exemplifies. His statement gains force from being voiced to her while he is puzzling her by wanting to feel something strongly. In answer to her pat, "When the individual feels, the community reels," he comes out with, "Well, why shouldn't it reel a bit?" Then after her horrified protest, he goes on unabashed:

> "Adults intellectually and during working hours . . . Infants where feeling and desire are concerned."
> "Our Ford loved infants."
> Ignoring the interruption, "It suddenly struck me the other day," continued Bernard, "that it might be possible to be an adult all the time." (p. 110)

He feels "embattled against the order of things" as he listens to the rebuke about his behavior after working hours from the Director:

> "Alphas are so conditioned that they do not *have* to be infantile in their emotional behaviour. But that is all the more reason for their making a special effort to conform. It is their duty to be infantile, even against their inclination. And so, Mr. Marx, I give you fair warning." The Director's voice vibrated with an indignation that had now become wholly righteous and impersonal—was the expression of the disapproval of Society itself. "If ever I hear again of any lapse from a proper standard of infantile decorum, I shall ask for your transference to a Sub-Centre—preferably to Iceland. Good morning." (p. 115)

Bernard's continued resistance emphasizes the emptiness of the usual amusements. He is never shown playing Obstacle Golf or Centrifugal Bumble-Puppy, nor going to the feelies to have his senses tickled.

The corollary of the insistence on infantilism is the refusal to admit the realities of old age or even of death. Lenina sees her first honestly old person on the Savage Reservation; and Bernard has to explain to her that what she thinks of as old age in the Director is artificially created youth, achieved by keeping the metabolism permanently stimulated: "Youth almost unimpaired till sixty, and then, crack! the end." (p. 129) The climax of the insensibility of these grown-up people who emotionally might still be in their bottles comes with the death scene in the Park Lane Hospital for the Dying. For the perception of their attitude toward death, Huxley uses the consciousness of the Savage brought back by Bernard and Lenina from the reservation. John, the Savage, is the son of the Director and Linda, who has been a worker in the Fertilizing Room. Huxley achieves an extension of the allegorical effect by making the child, who has grown up on the reservation, the result of just such a holiday as Bernard and Lenina are taking, though the Director, embarrassed at having mentioned his trip to Bernard, says, "Don't imagine . . . that I'd had any indecorous relation with the girl. Nothing emotional, nothing long-drawn." (p. 114) The interlude of the visit to the reservation gives Huxley a chance to depict a primitive society in contrast to his utopian one and also allows Bernard to bring John and Linda back. At the same time it further reveals Bernard since his invitation to them springs entirely from motives of self-aggrandizement: he wishes to confound the Director by confronting him with Linda and to give himself importance by producing John for study. He does, in fact, achieve a brief splendor and can list among the notables at his evening parties to meet the Savage, the chief Bottler, the Director of Predestination, three Deputy Assistant Fertilizer-Generals, the Professor of Feelies in the College of Emotional Engineering, the Dean of Westminster Community Singery, the Supervisor of Bokanovskification; and on the evening of his downfall he has added the Arch Community Songster of Canterbury. But in addition to revealing Bernard's pettiness, the Savage's presence in London, where he becomes a social lion, gives him a chance to react for the enlightenment of the reader to what he observes there. Huxley partly explains his point of view by his education. He has been taught to read by his mother out of her manual, *The Chemical and Bacteriological Conditioning of the Embryo. Practical Instructions for Beta Embryo-Store Workers;* but her instruction has ended with the nursery rhymes: "A, B, C, Vitamin D, The fat's in the liver, the cod's in the sea," and "Streptocock-Gee to Banbury T, to see a fine bathroom and W. C." His real enlightenment has come from a battered copy of *The Complete Works of William Shakespeare,* which has been found on the reservation in an ancient chest. His being possessed by the beauty of the poetry and the standards of behavior which he has found in Shakespeare helps to explain his separateness from both societies in which he must move; but he is not a wholly credible character. As Huxley points out in the foreword written for the edition of 1946, "For the sake . . . of dramatic effect, the Savage is often permitted to speak more rationally than his upbringing among the practitioners of a religion that is half fertility cult and half *Penitente* ferocity would actually warrant. Even his acquaintance with Shakespeare would not in reality justify such utterances." But his horror at the spurious emotion of the feelies, where he "feels" THREE WEEKS IN A HELICOPTER AN ALL-SUPERSINGING, SYNTHETIC-TALKING, COLOURED, STEREOSCOPIC FEELY. WITH SYNCHRONIZED SCENT-ORGAN ACCOMPANIMENT and at Lenina's attempts to seduce him after he has worshiped her with Miranda's wonder and longed to do something to make him worthy of her beauty and purity, does indeed give dramatic effect to the disillusion.

John provides the angle of vision from which Huxley presents the conception of death when Linda dies. What makes the episode desolating to him is not the grief he feels at the loss of his mother, though to the amazement and embarrassment of these decanted people, for whom the word *mother* is an obscenity, he does feel affection for her. It is the refusal to allow death its dignity, and grief any existence at all that makes him feel degraded. The reader, with him, is affronted first at the appearance of the building with its sixty-story tower of primrose tiles and the gaily colored aerial hearses that he sees as he leaves his taxicopter. The dismay grows as he is taken into the room, "bright with sunshine and yellow paint," where Linda is dying in bed twenty, along with the occupants of the other nineteen beds, to the accompaniment of television and synthetic music; and the nurse explains, "we try to create a thoroughly pleasant atmosphere here—something between a first-class hotel and a feely-palace, if you take my meaning." (p. 238) Even here he could have established some relation with Linda and with the old reality between them if it had not been for the intrusion of a bokanovsky group of children being death-conditioned:

> What seemed an interminable stream of identical eight-year-old male twins was pouring into the room. Twin after twin, twin after twin, they came—a nightmare. Their faces, their repeated face—for there was only one between the lot of them—puggishly stared, all nostrils and pale goggling eyes. Their uniform was khaki. All their mouths hung open. Squealing and chattering they entered. In a moment, it seemed, the ward was maggoty with them. They swarmed between the beds, clambered over, crawled under, peeped into the television boxes, made faces at the patients. (p. 241)

Huxley relentlessly presses home the violation of decency as the scene progresses. When John tries to drive the children away from Linda's bed, the nurse engages them in a game of hunt-the-zipper; but he breaks into it to fetch help when Linda actually dies. None of the reproofs of the nurses can bring the Savage to a proper sense of what the commotion he is causing may do to damage the responses of the "little ones," and they have to be given chocolate éclairs to keep their death-conditioning from being wrecked entirely. When John "in the chaos of grief and remorse" that fills his mind whispers "God," he is immediately surrounded again by curious children. "The Savage violently started and, uncovering his face, looked round. Five khaki twins, each with the stump of a long éclair in his right hand, and their identical faces variously smeared with liquid chocolate, were standing in a row, puggily goggling at him." (p.

248) No wonder the Savage leaves and in the hall creates a riot by throwing away the *soma* ration being distributed to the Delta workers by the Deputy Sub-Bursar.

One other consciousness which Huxley uses to reveal the society he is depicting, that of Helmholtz Watson, is almost human. Since Helmholtz is a perfect physical specimen and his sense of individuality is produced by mental excess, he is entirely without Bernard's self-defensive attitude. "By profession he was a lecturer at the College of Emotional Engineering (Department of Writing) and in the intervals of his educational activities, a working Emotional Engineer. He wrote regularly for *The Hourly Radio,* composed feely scenarios, and had the happiest knack for slogans and hypnopaedic rhymes." (p. 79) Huxley shows him bored with his success and longing to find something worth writing about, some substance to put behind his "piercing phrases." He is used partly in the displaying of Bernard, since it is especially in front of him that Bernard feels the compulsion to boast or to justify himself. His nevertheless remaining sincerely Bernard's friend shows that there is one person in this world of the future who retains a sense of values which will not disappoint the Savage completely. Thus when John does come, he instinctively chooses Helmholtz for a friend. Though the affinity between Helmholtz and the Savage fills Bernard with jealous rage, which drives him to shame and *soma,* among the three of them there is something which might have enabled each of them to become a person in a world where any man was free to become himself.

But Huxley is true to the imaginative terms he has laid down in not letting this happen. He is following the logic of his situation in having all three of the young men banished for being already too nearly human. He achieves another exposition of the principles of his society from within its imaginative structure when the Controller explains why it cannot tolerate them. The oratory of Mustapha Mond is "almost up to synthetic standards," as he declares, "We believe in happiness and stability. A society of Alphas couldn't fail to be unstable and miserable. Imagine a factory staffed by Alphas—that is to say by separate and unrelated individuals of good heredity and conditioned so as to be capable (within limits) of making a free choice and assuming responsibilities. Imagine it!" (p. 266) Huxley enforces the satire by letting it be Mustapha Mond who explains the proper attitude toward science. The Controller, who himself has sacrificed his love of pure science, which would have sent him too to an island, for a place on the Controllers' Council, which has led to his present position, declares: "Our Ford himself did a great deal to shift the emphasis from truth and beauty to comfort and happiness. Mass production demanded the shift. Universal happiness keeps the wheels steadily turning; truth and beauty can't." (p. 273)

When the three young men meet again before they all depart, they are happy in their sadness, for "their sadness was the symptom of their love for one another." (p. 291) It is a good omen; but Huxley does not allow us to see the achievement of manhood on the part of any one of them. Helmholtz and Bernard must be off to their islands; and the Savage, before he achieves his attempted purgation, is driven to suicide by the prying crowds who surge in upon his privacy much as the curious twins in the hospital had done. For them his self-flagellations are simply the stunt with the whip, a more exciting sensation even than can be obtained at the feelies. It is his inevitable fate in a world where, as Huxley says in his foreword, the minds of the people are "purged of all the natural decencies," where stability has been achieved by making them love their servitude and hypnotizing them into the belief that "Everybody's happy nowadays."

Huxley's slave state is posited on the assumption set forth in the foreword to the new edition of *Brave New World:* "A really efficient totalitarian state would be one in which the all-powerful executive of the political bosses and their army of managers control a population of slaves who do not have to be coerced, because they love their servitude. To make them love it is the task assigned." In the world he depicts, the task has been accomplished. The "problem of happiness" has been solved.

The theory of power on which George Orwell bases his world in *Nineteen Eighty-four* achieves slavery on opposite principles. Power is asserted by making the individual suffer. "Obedience is not enough," says the dictator to Winston Smith. "Unless he is suffering, how can you be sure that he is obeying your will and not his own? Power is in inflicting pain and humiliation. Power is in tearing human minds to pieces and putting them together again in new shapes of your own choosing. . . . Progress in our world will be progress toward more pain. . . . Always, at every moment, there will be the thrill of victory, the sensation of trampling on an enemy who is helpless. If you want a picture of the future, imagine a boot stamping on a human face—forever." [4]

The essential difference in the methods of destroying humanity in the two future societies is closely linked with the difference in the aspects of our time being allegorized. In *Brave New World* Huxley's vehicle is an extension of our love of comfort made possible by material development and the consequent drugging of our human faculties. In *Nineteen Eighty-four* Orwell's is an extension of the political terrorization which we now see in practice. There is perhaps a connection between the fundamental suppositions in the tenors; and they lead to identical conclusions of the destruction of man's dignity. But the destroying process is different,

4. (New York, 1949), pp. 269–71. All quotations are from this edition.

though even it has similar elements such as the complete lack of privacy, the control of thought, and the abolition of history.

The structure of Orwell's book is more sharply defined than that of *Brave New World,* for the greater violence of his terms demands an organization that is dramatic in its impact. It would seem melodramatic if it did not have such an ominous ring of truth. Its three divisions are like the three acts of a play. In the first, there is a masterly exposition of what *1.* life in the society is like as it affects Winston Smith, who is miserably struggling to achieve some sense of himself, trying to preserve his sanity and wondering if "Perhaps a lunatic was simply a minority of one."

2. (p. 80) In the second, there is the dramatic development in which he manages against tremendous odds to achieve a real experience of love with a girl who hates the Party as much as he does and, without understanding the meaning of unorthodoxy, is immensely clever at managing to stay alive: "She spent an astonishing amount of time in attending lectures and demonstrations, distributing literature for the Junior Anti-Sex League, preparing banners for Hate Week, making collections for the savings campaign, and suchlike activities. It paid, she said; it was camouflage. If you kept the small rules you could break the big ones." (p. 130) In spite of Julia's gift for survival, they have both known since they began to commit Thoughtcrime that they had better think of themselves as dead; and the curtain of the second act comes as Winston says, daring to think of the future, "We are the dead." Julia echoes, "We are the dead," and an iron voice behind them pronounces their doom, "You are the dead." (p. 222) Orwell has increased the anxiety for them throughout this section by showing the interplay of their sense of doom and their clinging to what they have achieved of a feeling of security—almost of domesticity. They have known that they must be caught; but they have allowed themselves moments of the illusion of safety and of belonging to each other rather than to Big Brother, the symbol of the Party, because under that illusion something that they felt to be real could grow. Now it is over; and the third act, Winston's "cure," is begun. It does not end until he has learned that "He loved Big Brother."

3 Besides the tight dramatic structure, another means of intensification in *Nineteen Eighty-four* is the focusing of attention exclusively on Winston's perceptions. This concentration on a single point of view is as skillfully managed as is the revolving point of view in *Brave New World* and as proper for the purpose in hand. Winston's awareness becomes our awareness; and we suffer with him. We feel the outward discomfort and ugliness of the life he must lead; and we share his inner bewilderment and pain. Orwell makes clear that we are to feel with Winston's senses from the opening paragraph: "It was a bright cold day in April, and the clocks were striking thirteen. Winston Smith, his chin nuzzled into his breast in an effort to escape the vile wind, slipped quickly through the doors of Victory Mansions, though not quickly enough to prevent a swirl of gritty dust from entering along with him." (p. 3) Through his senses we smell the hall smell of boiled cabbage and old rags, see the huge picture with the eyes that follow everyone and the caption BIG BROTHER IS WATCHING YOU, and hear the fruity voice reading figures from the telescreen. We are chagrined when the tobacco falls out of his carefully guarded VICTORY CIGARETTES if he forgets to hold them horizontal; we are affronted at the Parsons' apartment which looks "as though the place had just been visited by some large violent animal" (p. 22); we shudder at the greasy tray and the gravy-streaked table in the canteen, and at the "sourish, composite smell of bad gin and bad coffee and metallic stew and dirty clothes." (p. 60) We share his protest: "was it not a sign that this was *not* the natural order of things, if one's heart sickened at the discomfort and dirt and scarcity, the interminable winters, the stickiness of one's socks, the lifts that never worked, the cold water, the gritty soap, the cigarettes that came to pieces, the food with its strange evil tastes? Why should one feel it to be intolerable unless one had some kind of ancestral memory that things had once been different?" The people who surround him are as sharply contrasted with the inhabitants of Huxley's utopia as his world itself is with Fordian comfort, though the Party ideal of physique might have been modeled on the products of the decanting bottles in the Hatcheries:

> How easy it was, thought Winston, if you did not look about you, to believe that the physical type set up by the Party as an ideal—tall muscular youths and deep-bosomed maidens, blond-haired, vital, sunburnt, carefree—existed and even predominated. Actually, so far as he could judge, the majority of people in Airstrip One were small, dark, and ill-favored. It was curious how that beetlelike type proliferated in the Ministries: little dumpy men, growing stout very early in life, with short legs, swift scuttling movements, and fat inscrutable faces with very small eyes. It was the type that seemed to flourish best under the dominion of the Party. (pp. 60–1)

What is most intolerable to Winston in the life he has to live is the complete lack of privacy. This degradation too we share with him, so uncannily is the feeling conveyed of the ubiquitous telescreens which pick up every movement and every sound above a whisper, at the same time that they transmit the Party propaganda or the directions for the Physical Jerks, through which Winston must push his aching frail body after the ear-splitting whistle from the telescreen has made him wrench himself out of bed. Orwell uses two of man's most private acts, keeping a diary and love-making, to show the futility of Winston's efforts to achieve any citadel against the prying of the state. The deed by which he is about to try to discover himself as a person when the book opens is the starting of a diary, for which he has been rash enough to buy at an old junk shop a fifty-year-old book of beautiful creamy paper.

He was a lonely ghost uttering a truth that nobody would ever hear. But so long as he uttered it, in some obscure way the continuity was not broken. It was not by making yourself heard but by staying sane that you carried on the human heritage. He went back to the table, dipped his pen, and wrote:

To the future or to the past, to a time when thought is free, when men are different from one another and do not live alone—to a time when truth exists and what is done cannot be undone:

From the age of uniformity, from the age of solitude, from the age of Big Brother, from the age of doublethink—greetings! (pp. 28–29)

We are inside Winston's consciousness in his realization that this is Thoughtcrime and that Thoughtcrime is death and in the care he takes to conceal himself from the telescreen to do his writing and to place a piece of dust on the cover of his diary so that he can tell if it has been molested. But Orwell manages a highly effective double consciousness for the reader: while we participate with Winston in his efforts to escape detection, to stay alive exactly because he realizes that he is a dead man, we see with a greater clairvoyance than he achieves, the futility of his present precautions. Big Brother is watching.

There is the same sort of ghostly presence hovering behind all the carefully contrived assignations with Julia. It is days after her first sign before Winston manages to say a single word to her. But when it is uttered, Orwell makes us know without telling us, that it has been overheard. As the lovers lose themselves in the crowds of the streets, walking never abreast, but sometimes achieving a few hasty words; when they actually meet in the woods, in the abandoned tower, and finally in the room which Winston has recklessly rented above the junk shop—all the while we share their own apprehension, indeed their sure knowledge, that they will be caught and "vaporized." But we also feel an apprehension for and beyond them, a sense of tragic concern for their fate, of which Orwell succeeds in making us foretaste the horror more clearly than they do themselves.

Possibly Winston has as a character something of the defect that Huxley points out in the Savage, of possessing a greater awareness of the meaning of human self-respect than he could possibly have acquired from his experience; but we do not make this criticism while we are entering into his strivings. Orwell successfully uses his point of view to communicate the quality of the life around him as he longs to achieve some other emotion than that generated by the daily two minutes' hate, when the picture of Emmanuel Goldstein as the primal traitor is used to whip up a rage that becomes abstract and can be turned in any direction, or the still more violent measures that are used to arouse the frenzy of Hate Week. His seeking for the kind of emotion that will make him feel human is part of what makes him convincing as a character. What disturbs him most deeply is what seems to him the "truly characteristic thing about modern life . . . not its cruelty and insecurity, but simply its bareness, its dinginess, its listlessness." (p. 73) He has loathed his visit to an ancient prostitute among the "proles" as much as the mechanical embraces of his former wife, who has compelled him to go through the weekly performance of trying to produce a child for the Party, though her rigid body seemed to push him off while she clasped him to her. Consorting with prostitutes is forbidden by the Party, but not severely punished: "Mere debauchery did not matter very much, so long as it was furtive and joyless, and only involved the women of a submerged and despised class. . . . The aim of the Party was not merely to prevent men and women from forming loyalties which it might not be able to control. Its real, undeclared purpose was to remove all pleasure from the sexual act." (p. 65) Julia understands all this much more clearly than Winston does: "Unlike Winston, she had grasped the inner meaning of the Party's sexual puritanism. It was not merely that the sex instinct created a world of its own which was outside the Party's control and which therefore had to be destroyed if possible. What was more important was that sexual privation induced hysteria, which was desirable because it could be transformed into war fever and leader worship." (p. 134)

The war, which is one of Orwell's most pervasive symbols of enslavement, is continuous, with shifts of enmity and alliance between Eurasia and Eastasia for the land mass of Oceania, which Winston and Julia inhabit. Its effects are everywhere: in Winston's duty at the Ministry of Truth, or Minitrue as it is in Newspeak, to rewrite history so as to obliterate the shifts of enemy and ally; in the victory news which precedes announcements of cuts in the ersatz chocolate ration or some other goods like razor blades or shoe strings that are in short supply; in the bombs which drop at intervals without causing disastrous destruction so that the proles have learned just to drop to the ground or rush to shelter when an animal-like instinct tells them that one is coming; in the dust which swirls in the bomb sites, where rubble is simply left in heaps. The theory of the slogan WAR IS PEACE is expounded in the book supposedly by Goldstein and the basis of a subversive brotherhood, but actually by O'Brien, the leader of the Party, and given to Winston by O'Brien to complete his undoing:

It is a warfare of limited aims between combatants who are unable to destroy one another, have no material cause for fighting, and are not divided by any genuine ideological difference. . . . In centers of civilization war means no more than a continuous shortage of consumption goods, and the occasional crash of a rocket bomb which may cause a few score of deaths. . . . To understand the nature of the present war—for in spite of the regrouping which occurs every few years, it is always the same war—one must realize in the first place that it is impossible for it to be decisive. (pp. 186–7)

The war not only determines the physical environment, but contributes to the various means by which the Party controls thought. The penalty for Thoughtcrime is arrest, always at night, by the Thought Police and then vaporization: "Your name was removed from the registers, every record of everything you had ever done was wiped out, your one-time existence was denied and then forgotten. You were abolished, annihilated: *vaporized* was the usual word." (p. 20) With Winston we watch the destruction of Rutherford and his companions Jones and Aaronson, the last of the original revolutionaries to be denounced as traitors by the Thought Police. Nobody ever escapes these instruments of the Party, whose object is to prevent Thoughtcrime. "The heresy of heresies was common sense. . . . The Party told you to reject the evidence of your eyes and ears. It was their final, most essential command." (pp. 80–1) Orwell gives a demonstration of their power in Winston himself. What dismays him as he starts out on his quest for sanity is the impossibility of knowing that they are wrong: "what was terrifying was not that they would kill you for thinking otherwise, but that they might be right. For, after all, how do we know that two and two make four? Or that the force of gravity works? Or that the past is unchangeable? If both the past and the external world exist only in the mind, and if the mind itself is controllable—what then?" (p. 80) His reflection that Comrade Ogilvy, whose exploits he has just created, exists "as authentically, and upon the same evidence, as Charlemagne or Julius Caesar" (p. 48) startles the reader, as it does Winston himself. Again Winston's enlightenment is communicated when he reads in the book O'Brien has given him that

> *Doublethink* means the power of holding two contradictory beliefs in one's mind simultaneously, and accepting both of them. The Party intellectual knows in which direction his memories must be altered; he therefore knows that he is playing tricks with reality; but by the exercise of *doublethink* he also satisfies himself that reality is not violated. The process has to be conscious, or it would not be carried out with sufficient precision, but it also has to be unconscious, or it would bring with it a feeling of falsity and hence of guilt. (p. 215)

The supreme example of *doublethink* is Engsoc, the name of the Party, since "the Party rejects and vilifies every principle for which the Socialist movement originally stood, and it chooses to do this in the name of Socialism." (p. 217)

The most appalling symbol of thought control is the abolition of history, which is vastly more thoroughgoing than in *Brave New World,* for the Party has not only destroyed records of the prerevolutionary past; it is constantly in the process of reconstructing the records of the immediate past to make them fit the Party line. This is forcibly brought out through Winston's work in Minitrue, which consists in "rectifying" such records as the speeches of Big Brother to make them fit what has happened, or the production figures announced as accomplished to adjust to those announced in advance (neither set having any relation to actual production).

> As soon as all the corrections which happened to be necessary in any particular number of the *Times* had been assembled and collated, that number would be reprinted, the original copy destroyed, and the corrected copy placed on the files in its stead. This process of continuous alteration was applied not only to newspapers, but to books, periodicals, pamphlets, posters, leaflets, films, sound tracks, cartoons, photographs—to every kind of literature or documentation which might conceivably hold any political or ideological significance. Day by day and almost minute by minute the past was brought up to date. In this way every prediction made by the Party could be shown by documentary evidence to have been correct; nor was any item of news, or any expression of opinion, which conflicted with the needs of the moment, ever allowed to remain on record. (pp. 40–1)

In fact, the *memory holes* through which all incriminating signs of the actual past are dropped to the oblivion of the destroying furnaces become a recurring concrete symbol of the destruction of memory, of the records of the long struggle of the race to emerge into humanity. The words *memory hole* have not suffered the mutilation of *Newspeak;* but they are as good an example of *doublethink* as Minitrue, Minipax, Miniluv, and Miniplenty, the names for the Ministry of Truth, which works at falsification; the Ministry of Peace, which deals with war; the Ministry of Love, which is the police; and the Ministry of Plenty, which manages rationing.

In contrast to the *memory holes,* there are some authentic symbols of the past. Among them are Winston's repeated recollections of his mother, who even in the poverty and persecution that had taken possession of the world before her vaporization, had tried to give him some sense of human decencies. The chief objective symbol of the past for him is the little paper weight with a flower of coral enclosed in "soft, rainwatery glass." (p. 95) He cherishes it the more because of its apparent uselessness, as signifying a time when men could love beauty itself. Orwell uses it with sinister effect, for like the whole junk shop and the shabby, old-fashioned room with its big double bed (appropriately vermin infested), it is a decoy to lure Winston further and irretrievably into Thoughtcrime. At the time of his arrest, it is wantonly, and again symbolically, dashed to pieces on the hearthstone. "The fragment of coral, a tiny crinkle of pink like a sugar rosebud from a cake, rolled across the mat. How small, thought Winston, how small it always was!" (p. 224)

There are other ironic symbols which evoke the real past and thus betray Winston by appealing to his sense of an actual earlier time. Part of the elaborate trap laid with diabolical insight into the way his yearning for association with the human can be used to betray him, is the nursery rhyme he learns from the man who is acting the part of the old junk shop tender. The steel engraving of St. Clement's Dane, which conceals the treacherous telescreen, seems to Winston to suggest the very essence of the atmosphere of the room—as it all too surely does. Part of the effect is the nursery rhyme, "Oranges and lemons, say the bells of St. Clement's," which the old man teaches him as they first look at it. As the rhyme repeatedly recurs to him, it seems to bring to his ears the actual sound of the church bells of the past. Though he does not complete all the intervening lines until O'Brien fills out his knowledge after his arrest, we shudder as the old man teaches him at once the premonitory last line: "Here comes a chopper to chop off your head."

There are other symbols used throughout the book in various ways. The whole life of the proles is largely symbolically suggested by the party slogan, "Proles and animals are free," and Winston's own, "If there is any hope it lies in the proles," of which he realizes the almost ludicrous irony. His walk in the slums, where the dwellings suggest rat holes and two bloated women fight over a flimsy saucepan which breaks in their hands, seems to gather up in one representation the sense of the life of violence and misery, where crime does not matter to the authorities "since it all happened among the proles themselves." (p. 72) His futile effort to learn from the old man in the pub whether the textbook teaching about capitalists who wore top hats and drank champagne is true, has the same representational quality. And the woman in the courtyard of his hideout goes back and forth hanging up diapers and singing a cloyingly sentimental song with the persistence of a Madame Defarge.

There are few characters who exist as individuals beyond Winston and Julia, for the good reason that we see people through his eyes, and it is impossible for him to tell whether there are others who share his yearning toward the status of persons. Two contrasting Party types are represented by Syme and Parsons. Syme is the intellectual who has a "pedant's passion" for Newspeak, which he is helping to put into final shape. "It's a beautiful thing, the destruction of words," he says to Winston as he explains that there is no need for the word *bad* if we have *ungood,* nor for words like "splendid" and "excellent" when *plus good* covers the meaning. "In an intellectual way, Syme was venomously orthodox."

(pp. 50–2) But Winston knows that he will be vaporized; and pretty soon he vanishes. The list of the Chess Committee becomes one name shorter: "Syme had ceased to exist; he had never existed." (p. 140) His opposite is Parsons, the stupid devotee who takes a child's delight in the most adolescent of the Party activities, swallows avidly the Party propaganda, loves its slogans and parades, and is proud of its success in turning his children into little monsters. His lack of imagination appears in his boasting of his girl's having brought about the arrest and probable death of a man whom she has spotted as wearing a "funny kind of shoes" so that he is obviously a foreigner and therefore a spy. "Pretty smart for a nipper of seven, eh?" (p. 58) Parsons is still proud of her when she has denounced him. He is a pathetic figure when Winston encounters him in prison, blubbering out his loyalty to the Party: *"You* know what kind of a chap I was. Not a bad chap in my way. Not brainy, of course, but keen. I tried to do my best for the Party, didn't I?" (p. 236) His simplicity is shown in his being convinced that the insidious Thoughtcrime has possessed his mind in his sleep and that he is truly guilty. In answer to Winston's question as to who denounced him, he says, "It was my little daughter . . . She listened at the keyhole. Heard what I was saying, and nipped off to the patrols the very next day. Pretty smart for a nipper of seven, eh? I don't bear her any grudge for it. In fact I'm proud of her. It shows I brought her up in the right spirit, anyway." (p. 237) There are other briefly and sharply etched people in the cells, such as the poet Ampleforth, who has been condemned because in his rewriting of Kipling he has left the word God at the end of a line; but these too are types.

The only other extended characterization is that of O'Brien, the villain of the piece. It is part of the melodramatic quality of the work that he is made completely inhuman. His being devoid of feeling is appropriate to the whole conception; but Orwell gives him too omniscient a diabolical cleverness to win belief, though we believe in what he makes Winston undergo. We feel physically and mentally assaulted by the horrors of the whole third act, which is taken up with his "cure" of Winston. As the rats approach Winston's face in Room 101, which stands for the one unendurable thing in the imagination of each prisoner, we understand the revulsion that makes him commit the final disloyalty and cry out, "Do it to Julia!" (p. 289) We have already felt the bodily pain that wracks him as O'Brien carefully controls the degrees needed to make him acknowledge that four is five. Since one of the early entries in his diary had been: *"Freedom is the freedom to say that two plus two make four"* (p. 81), we are shattered as he loses this freedom. What Winston experiences, we are compelled to feel. But we never quite believe in O'Brien as the all-knowing, all-comprehending fiend, who nevertheless spends infinite time and trouble to find out just the ways to take possession of Winston's be-

ing and bring him finally to the love of Big Brother. Would the head of
the state bother to spend hours instructing Winston in *doublethink?*
Would he arrange so carefully the long drawn torture that wrecks his
victim physically and mentally and then the careful healing of his body
to destroy his soul? O'Brien is a vivid incarnation of evil; but he is not
a convincing character as head of the police state. And since these are the
given terms of the allegory, the failure to win belief in O'Brien is an
allegorical defect. Orwell's indictment becomes more somber, more
dreadful, and more convincing after the scenes of torture are over when
we go through the ginsoaked days of the listless Winston, who is now
incapable of any emotion except love of Big Brother: "Two gin-scented
tears trickled down the sides of his nose. But it was all right, everything
was all right, the struggle was finished. He had won the victory over
himself. He loved Big Brother." (p. 300)

8

Conclusion

"the pleasure of concernment"
JOHN DRYDEN

"the pleasure of ulteriority"
ROBERT FROST

IF THE foregoing analyses of examples have at all served their purpose, several conclusions have emerged concerning the art they exemplify. The primary object of the discussions has been to show the working of the artistic process; but since the art in question is the delivering of a moral judgment, one of the most striking impressions that grows out of an extended consideration of its practice is the consistency of intention behind it. The common aim of the writers reviewed is to quicken in some way man's sense of himself as man. They vindicate the statement of Phillips Brooks that "All satire must keep sight of man's greatness." [1] The complaint against satire that it springs from hostility as a motive, fails to take account of the direction of the hostility, which operates against some defection of man from his humanity. Thus the satiric reproof implies a positive standard which has its source in man's own nature. Furthermore, satire does man the honor of holding him capable of self-scrutiny. It is true that there are more exalted forms of art; but the object of satire is not the degradation of man. Rather it is to show him the ways in which he has degraded himself. If the pictures the satirists paint of imagined evils are sickening, it is because of the recognition in them of real evils.

Another conclusion which springs from the examination of examples is that allegory need not be dull. By its very nature it presupposes an imaginative act on the part of the reader to correspond to the artist's act of creative imagination. Its power to engage such participation is in strict proportion to the writer's imaginative power and the reader's in response. Allegory is one of the most exacting of forms; but when its principles suggested in Chapter 1 are followed, it is one of the most exciting. The

1. Alexander V. G. Allen, *Life and Letters of Phillips Brooks* (New York, 1900), *2*, 819.

zest may depend basically upon the intellectual game of solving a riddle; but while this pleasure is always present, it is also transcended in the best allegories. The delight becomes the complex imaginative one of having the truth take on an extra dimension because of the reticence and the controlled precision of the indirection with which it is revealed. Shapes seen through a veil or a mist are more interesting than those exposed in the glare of direct light.

Thus the examples reveal something of the nature of satire and something of the nature of allegory. They show still more of the nature of satiric allegory. If a work in this genre is successful, it must succeed as both satire and allegory; and its success as one depends on its success as the other. The failures that have been treated are perhaps the clearest proof of this: *Mother Hubberds Tale* is passionate satire, but it fails as a work of art because the satire is not allegorically realized; *News from Nowhere* keeps fairly clearly to its allegorical frame, but the insipidity of the satire makes the allegory uninteresting. If the allegorical satire is to exist as a work of art, the fusion must be so complete that we have the feeling of the satire's having been actually conceived as allegory. It is fatal to the effect to give the impression either that the writer thought out his criticism and then decided to pour it into an allegorical mold or that he decided to write an allegory and then chose the criticism to give it point. Like any other work of art, the satiric allegory must exist as an organic unity: tenor and vehicle must so interanimate one another that they seem to belong inevitably together. The number of satiric allegories which have this sort of inevitability demonstrates the affinity between satire and allegory. An attempt was made in Chapter 1 to explain the reasons for the affinity. All of the forces of sympathy there set forth, from common need for indirection and compression to common concern for judgment, have been shown operating in particular writings. Where they are in full play, the result is a work of art possessing its own integrity and a tensile strength which is increased by the salutary interplay of the satire with the allegory.

The genre is one of variety and extent limited only by the range of man's defections from the ideal with which the satirist is concerned and by the power of the artist to give his concern expression in allegory. If the impetus that disturbs the author into writing is a single fault of man, he can impale his imagined victim in a single episode, as Dryden does in *Mac Flecknoe;* if the loss of a sense of values by a whole society is what troubles him, he must create a whole imagined society to carry his indictment, as Huxley and Orwell do in *Brave New World* and *Nineteen Eighty-four*. The allegorical structures are as multitudinous as the faults of man which they satirize. They afford all manner of strange shapes which haunt the imagination and tease us not "out of thought" but into it. Such variety is part of the richness of the form, which makes it claim critical attention, and part of the pleasure in it, though this is not to acknowledge pleasure in the variety of evil on which it depends.

The whole question of the reader's pleasure in satire is a thorny and complex one, finally as unsolvable as that of tragic pleasure—and allied to it. Satire, like tragedy, is a way of taking seriously man's condition. It is a recognition of the unending conflict between his baseness and his greatness. The satirist who sees allegorically has an especially vivid way of sharing with the reader the doubleness of his vision, interpreting at once the standard by which he judges and man's defection from the standard. There is exhilaration, however painful, in the exercise of judgment which gives point to the view of evil. There is also for creator and reader alike the peculiar pleasure of the sheer exercise of the imaginative faculty, which operates with extraordinary power in this highly complex form. Satiric allegory seems especially adapted to express the paradox of the nature of man himself "created half to rise and half to fall."

Index

Absalom's Conspiracy: or, the Tragedy of Treason, 19

Addison, Joseph, *Spectator, 249,* 33

Aesop, 31; Fables, 57–8

African folk tales, 57

Allegorical satire: artistic process in, 135; consistency of intention in, 135; criteria for defining, 2; moral judgment in, 135; necessity of artistic unity in, 136. *See also* Satiric allegory

Allegory: action not essential to, 5; aesthetic appeal in, 4; ambiguity in meaning of, 2; as riddle, 6, 136; as sustained description, 5; as sustained metaphor, 5; attack of romantic critics on, 5; criteria for judging, 6; definition, 6; didactic function, 3, 4; difficulty of defining, 2; disparagement of, 1, 4; etymology, 2; four senses in medieval church, 3; elevation in, 4; indirection essential to, 4; interaction of tenor and vehicle in, 6; Johnson's definition of, 5; linking of personification with, 3, 4; means of making satire objective, 10; not dull, 135–6

Allegory and satire. *See* Satire and allegory

Allegories, medieval, 9, 13

Animal stories: absence of vivid human characters in, 60–1; aggregations of, governed by same rules as single stories, 61–2; as allegorical satire, 59; belief in animals, 60; brevity, 62; concentration on isolated human traits in, 61, 63; criteria for judging, 60–70; man's likeness to animals, 57; necessity of sustaining two levels in, 60; point of view in, 65–6; recognition of familiar in, 60; relation of tenor to vehicle in, 60; relationships among groups, 64–5; used for social satire, 66–70

Barclay, Alexander, *Shyp of Foles,* 8, 9, 56

Bellamy, Edward: more adult vision of future than Morris, 110; projection of ideas in *Looking Backward,* 110–14

Looking Backward, 107, 110–14; age and youth in, 113; allegory not sustained in, 114; brotherhood of man in,

112; classless society in, 113; community kitchen and dining hall in, 112–13; didacticism in, 111–14; military organization in, 112; production and distribution in, 111; separateness of story and idea in, 111–12

Bentley, Richard, 31, 33

Berdiaff, Nicolas, 114

Boyce, Benjamin, definition of Theophrastan character, 53

Boyle, Charles, 33

Breton, Nicholas, 53

Brooks, Phillips, 135

Bunyan, John, *Pilgrim's Progress,* 11, 12

Burke, Kenneth, 9

Butler, Joseph, *Analogy,* 95

Butler, Samuel (1612–80), procedure in *Hudibras,* 37–52; view of Puritans, 40

Characters, 37, 40, 48

Hudibras, 34, 37–52, 53, 95; allegorical method in, 37; angle of vision, distortion, in, 47, 49; attitude toward hero in, 47; chivalry in, 47; difficulty of scheme in, 41; faults in, 50–2; Hardin Craig's identification of bear baiters in, 44; impression of Hudibras, 41–3; Johnson's criticism of, 44–5, 47; loose structure in, 49–50; love story in, 46–7; ludicrous behavior of Hudibras, 44–6; moral purpose of, 39; presentation of bear baiters, 43–4; question of fairness, 46–8; Ralph, 43; relation of episodes to history, 49; speeches, 50–1; vehicle not entirely related to tenor, 48

"Miscellaneous Observations," 37

"Observations on Books and Authors," 38

Posthumous Works, 48

Butler, Samuel (1835–1902), procedure in *Erewhon,* 92–106

"Crossing the Rangitata," 93

"Darwin among the Machines," 103

Erewhon, 12, 92–106; abrupt shift to allegory in, 94; belief in health in, 97–8; Birth Formulae, 102; Book of the Machines, 92, 103; Colleges of Unreason, 102; exuberance in, 95–7; geography of, 93–4; Higgs's enlightenment in, 99; impression of narrative of exploration in, 92–4; irony in, 98; irrelevant details

YALE STUDIES IN ENGLISH

This volume is the one hundred and thirtieth of the Yale Studies in English, founded by Albert Stanburrough Cook in 1898 and edited by him until his death in 1927. Tucker Brooke succeeded him as editor, and served until 1941, when Benjamin C. Nangle succeeded him.

The following volumes are still in print. Orders should be addressed to YALE UNIVERSITY PRESS, New Haven, Connecticut.

120. WAITH, EUGENE M., The Pattern of Tragicomedy in Beaumont and Fletcher. $4.00.
121. MARSH, F., Wordsworth's Imagery. $3.75.
122. IRVING, E. B., JR. (Editor), The Old English *Exodus*. $5.00.
123. PRICE, MARTIN, Swift's Rhetorical Art. $3.75.
124. QUIRK, RANDOLPH, The Concessive Relation in Old English Poetry. $4.00.
125. MARTZ, L. L., The Poetry of Meditation. $5.00.
126. HOLDEN, WILLIAM P., Anti-Puritan Satire, 1572–1642. $3.75.
127. VOGEL, STANLEY M., German Literary Influences on the American Transcendentalists. $4.00.
128. FROST, WILLIAM, Dryden and the Art of Translation. $3.50.
129. BRADLEY, JOHN LEWIS, Ruskin's Letters from Venice, 1851–1852. $5.00.
130. LEYBURN, ELLEN DOUGLASS, Satiric Allegory. Mirror of Man. $3.00.